SO-AUD-033

The Mormon Landscape

The Mormon Landscape

Existence, Creation, and Perception
of a Unique Image
in the American West

Richard V. Francaviglia

AMS PRESS INC.
NEW YORK

First AMS Press edition: 1978

Library of Congress Cataloging in Publication Data.

Francaviglia, Richard V.
  The Mormon landscape.

  Bibliography: p
  Includes index
  1. Landscape assessment — Utah. 2. Man —
Influence on nature. 3. Mormons and Mormonism
in Utah. I Title.
GF91.U6F7   979.2   77-83791
ISBN 0-404-16020-4

Photographs and maps by R. V. Francaviglia.

Manufactured in the United States of America

AMS PRESS, INC.
NEW YORK, N.Y.

To our friends
Golden and Ada Oldroyd
of Nephi, Utah

Acknowledgments

Three groups of people deserve special mention for having made this study possible. First, the many Mormon townspeople and farmers who were so willing to discuss the role of the Latter-day Saints in changing the face of their land, the Mormon West. Second, the courteous and helpful people at the Historian's Office, Church of Jesus Christ of Latter-day Saints, and the Utah Historical Society, both in Salt Lake City, Utah, for making available many rare and precious documents. Third, and last, the University of Oregon: The Department of Geography, especially Professors E.T. Price, C.P. Patton and E. Smith; for their helpful comments, and Professor M. Donnelly of the Department of Art History, for her enlightening and helpful comments on Mormon architecture.

Contents

List of Illustrations

Figure *Page*

Introduction

For more than a century, common folk and scholars, both Mormon and non-Mormon, have commented on the religious and cultural impact of the Church of Jesus Christ of Latter-day Saints. There is little doubt that the Mormons have been an important group in the settlement of the Intermontane West. But even though several scholars have demonstrated that the morphology of Mormon towns and cities is unique,[1] a subject that has received little or no attention has been the role of the Mormons themselves in creating a distinctive landscape or visual setting in the West. The actual appearance of the village and rural cultural landscape—the totality of the real religious and folk elements such as chapels, homes, barns, gardens and fences, and their combinations—has not been dealt with in any clear or satisfactory manner.

Landscape, as used here, is an image of a place or area based upon some abstraction of reality, for it involves selection of certain elements as typical or significant. Another term which has been used for landscape in a very similar sense is "compage," although landscape is more restricted to the purely visual realm.[2]

Geographers have been slow, however, to explore the visual qualities of landscape. This is especially true of the Mormon landscape: Travelers have often noted that "something happens" when they approach Utah. They have intuitive feelings. "It is something about the houses," they may say.

But that "something" has remained undefined. Even Donald Meinig, in his fine analysis of the Mormon Culture Region, merely restated the mystery when he mentioned the Mormons' "visible imprint on the land," but explored it no further.[3] Likewise, the urban planner Charles Sellers noted that "anyone familiar with the historical geography of the United States knows that a sizeable portion of the Intermontane West bears the impress of Mormon culture."[4] Yet Sellers never defined "impress" in the sense of an image: Rather, he dealt with town planning. The German geographer Lautensach came closest to dealing with certain visual elements in the Mormon landscape, but his fascination with the Mormons as a cultural group precluded any detailed landscape investigation.[5] David Sopher's very brief analysis of the Mormons in his chapter "Religion and the Land" had tantalizing possibilities, but remained in an embryonic state as a mere paragraph of impressions.[6]

In short, visits to, and studies of, the Mormon West have been many, but, as George Perkins Marsh noted over a century ago, "sight is faculty; seeing, an art." Geographers have, as a rule, had their eyes closed to landscape. Little time and energy has been devoted to the study of landscape as art history which Leighly advocated many years ago.[7] Consequently, we know little about the visual heritage of cultural groups, especially in the United States. And we know next to nothing about the concept of religion as a motivating factor in the creation of landscapes. Only recently has this been even systematically investigated.[8]

Generally, studies of religious groups by geographers have tended toward spatial analysis of various movements.[9] These have been extremely important in setting a spatial framework, but have not yielded more than isolated clues about the role of the various groups as dynamic elements in the creation of landscapes. Such studies have been for the most part nonvisual, even though their authors may have had specific impressions of places settled by the groups studied.

Both geographers and common folk have, of course, had

some vivid impressions of Mormon Country; some true, some false. These types of impressions are very valuable, and were in fact the source of inspiration for my own study. For a cultural geographer, the questions they provoked were tantalizing: 1) Is there really a distinctive landscape associated with rural-village Mormon settlement? If so, what is it? 2) How do these elements vary in space and time? 3) What were the primary factors in creating such a landscape? 4) How have writers and artists attempted to render the visual composition that is the landscape? and 5) Are the Mormons themselves aware of any difference between Mormon and non-Mormon landscapes? The answers to these questions, it is hoped, will offer a significant contribution to the field of geography.

It was thus with much interest that an intensive six-month period of field investigation was undertaken from June to December, 1969. By 1965, the area vaguely defined by Wallace Stegner as "Mormon Country" had been given very specific spatial boundaries by geographer Donald Meinig.[10] That vast portion of the West called "Mormon Country," and later more specifically the "Mormon culture region," was studied by way of automobile, on foot, and on horseback. The results of that field work, which covered more than 13,000 actual miles, follow in this study of the Mormon landscape. It is for the most part within that vast region known as the Mormon Culture Region that a very special landscape exists. The elusive, but distinctive, concept "Mormon landscape" is exemplified by the village of Canaanville and its surroundings. The village provides a solid introduction to Mormon Country.

The traveler will not find the Mormon village of Canaanville on a map, however. Nor will the scholar find it in historical records. Canaanville exists in the mind as a vision of one of hundreds of small Mormon towns in the West. The town is hardly, however, the result of imagination; rather, it is a carefully generalized concept which emerged from detailed studies of Mormon towns. The description of Canaanville is a description of many a Mormon town.

NOTES

1. See, for example, L. Nelson, *The Mormon Village, A Pattern and Technique of Land Settlement* (Salt Lake City: University of Utah Press, 1952); and C. L. Sellers, "Early Mormon Community Planning," *Journal of the American Institute of Planners*, Vol. 28 (1962), pp. 24-30.

2. For discussion of landscape, see, for example, E. T. Price, "Viterbo: Landscape of an Italian City," *Annals, Association of American Geographers*, Vol. 54 (1964), pp. 242-275; and R. J. Solomon, "Procedures in Townscape Analysis," *Annals, Association of American Geographers*, Vol. 56 (1966), pp. 254-268. On "Compage," see D. Whittlesey, "The Regional Concept and the Regional Method," *American Geography—Inventory and Prospect*, ed. by Preston James and Clarence Jones (Syracuse: Syracuse University Press, 1954), pp. 46-47.

3. D. W. Meinig, "The Mormon Culture Region: Strategies and Patterns in the Geography of the American West, 1847-1964," *Annals, Association of American Geographers*, Vol. 55 (1965), p. 193.

4. Sellers, "Early Mormon Community Planning," p. 24.

5. H. Lautensach, *Das Mormonenland als Beispiel eines sozialsgeographischen Raumes* (Bonn: Im Selbstverlag des Geographischen Instituts der Universität Bonn, 1953).

6. D. Sopher, *Geography of Religions* (Englewood Cliffs: Prentice-Hall Inc., 1967), p. 45.

7. J. Leighly, "Some Comments on Contemporary Geographic Method," *Annals, Association of American Geographers*, Vol. 27 (1937) pp. 125-141.

8. E. Bjorklund, "Ideology and Culture Exemplified in Southwestern Michigan," *Annals, Association of American Geographers*, Vol. 54 (1964), pp. 227-241; also Sopher, *Geography of Religions*, pp. 24-46.

9. See, for example, W. Zelinsky, "An Approach to the Religious Geography of the United States," *Annals, Association of American Geographers*, Vol. 51 (1961), pp. 139-193; also Meinig, "The Mormon Culture Region."

10. W. Stegner, *Mormon Country* (New York: Duell, Sloane and Pearce, 1942); and Meinig, "The Mormon Culture Region."

PART I

Landscape of
the Latter-Day Saints

CHAPTER 1

The Mormon Landscape:
Appearances and Impressions

CANAANVILLE AND ENVIRONS

As persecution and flight are Mormon history, deliberate isolation in a harsh land called Zion is the crux of Mormon geography. Any description of Mormon country, therefore, must begin with the bold, semi-arid backdrop which frames all cultural elements. Canaanville can only be interpreted, economically, historically, and visually, in its rugged mountain-valley setting.

The floor of Canaan Valley itself lies almost a mile above sea level. The valley is north-south trending, a narrow crease about 6 miles wide and 30 miles long. It is not an enclosed valley; it drains southward into another, very similar in appearance. Canaan Valley is but one of many lying within the corrugated country that forms the eastern fringe of the Great Basin and the western edge of the Rocky Mountain chain.

The sagebrush- and cedar-peppered flanks of the surrounding hills and mountains rise another half mile to pine-covered summits which form a bold and irregular skyline at almost 8,000 feet. Aside from some timber exploitation, and a little stock driving, the mountains have remained almost unexploited. To Canaan Valley's residents they appear as solid sentinels, and with good reason: Not only are they perceived as offering a psychological security which we shall discuss later, but they are also very real orographic barriers running across the grain of the westerly air flow. In winter they are mantled with a carpet of snow which, somewhat delayed, later reaches to the valley floor. In summer, cumulus clouds pile up above their slopes, and later spread across the valley floor—much diminished in quantity and intensity. Their water supply is dependable, and reaches the valley by large canyons which enter at right angles. Except for lumber removal, these canyons have suffered little exploitation. The canyon behind Canaanville has, however, been dammed. But behind the small concrete dam, it remains choked with cottonwoods, box elders and other large trees, as well as smaller bushes. It disgorges onto the valley floor below by way of an impressive swelling alluvial fan. The fields and village below are watered by the main water course. Water is brought to field and village by a large canal or "big ditch," from which smaller ditches diverge, spreading water across the land in a grid pattern.

Citizens of Canaan Valley will always volunteer the information that their ancestors, the Mormon pioneers, "made the desert blossom as the rose." But in reality, Canaan Valley was not true desert in 1860 when the first settlers arrived: semi-arid conditions prevailed, and the pioneers re-directed water from dependable sources across the alluvial fans and gently sloping valley lands. The omnipresent silver-green of sagebrush retreated before the plow, and the emerald green of fields soon checkerboarded the valley land below. Indeed, beneath the towering hills and mountains lies a rural landscape at once striking to the traveler: Rectangular or square, golden or green, sharply defined patches of fields stretch before the eye. Most of these fields are pastures or hay lands. In a few parts of the valley, wheat and sugar beets are grown, but haying is dominant. Pastures and fields are intensively irrigated, crossed by smaller canals and ditches which are here and there lined by rows of Lombardy poplars and cottonwoods.

The erect, spire-like poplars vividly demarcate fields (Fig. 1). When in full foliage their dark green forms stand like

Figure 1.—Lombardy Poplar Reflected in Irrigation Ditch, Hinckley, Utah.

exclamation points against the somber gray-green of the mountains and the yellowish-green of fields; in fall they are yellow against fields of brown which have been tilled or harvested; in winter spindly bundles of crooked sticks stand out against the white of snow. Also seen are dead poplars, individuals or entire rows of them. Their grotesque, gnarled branches after a few years fall to the ground. Sometimes only a row of gray stumps remains, marking a dead and removed row of poplars or, occasionally, cottonwoods. The latter, when alive and healthy, are much the same color as the poplars, but have spreading crowns and thick trunks.

The fields and pastures with occasional rows of tall trees bordering them, are devoid of windmills, farmsteads, barns or other buildings. One may see agricultural equipment such as hay rakes and harrowers at the edge of the fields, but often the only signs of life will be stock grazing. Near Canaanville, as in much of Mormon country, one occasionally sees cattle and sheep grazing on the same pastures, a scene rarely encountered elsewhere.

The ubiquitous crooked and unpainted cedar post and barbed wire fence separates field from field, and field from road. Rarely a remnant of a stone wall may be seen, and "live fences" of sage or willows sometimes separate one hay field from another. In some places hay has been mowed and harvested into huge greenish-yellow piles—either loose or baled. These piles are set out for winter use, or to be later brought to town to feed stock kept there; sometimes the hay is sold to markets near larger cities or even out of state.

In Canaan Valley large wooden "hay derricks" dot the landscape (Fig. 2). These curious boom-and-stand implements are made of pine poles from the nearby mountains and, unpainted, are often bleached to a grayish color. They are used for stacking hay or loading hay onto trucks and hay wagons. Not many years ago horses were used for power, but today they are operated by a tractor which pulls the wire or cable

Figure 2.—Abandoned Hay Derrick near Levan, Utah.

attached to the short end of the cross pole. Pulleys are so arranged as to swing a full load of hay up off the ground and around, above the haystack or hay truck. Then the "jackson fork," which has secured the load, is "tripped," dropping the hay right into the desired location. Hay derricks are usually old implements, and many are no longer used due to the presence of newer mechanical conveyor hay bale loaders. Nevertheless, even if the derrick is not used, it remains in the landscape, its rope gone or some other vital part—such as a pulley —missing.

The open fields, semi-arid mountainous setting, irrigation ditches, and occasional rows of poplars and primitive fences lining fields give the rural landscape an almost biblical quality. Much as in some of the newer planned agricultural villages in Israel, Mormon farmers live in town and travel out to their fields during the daytime. Canaanville, of course, is a name that immediately brings forth biblical connotations; so are many of the names for real Mormon villages. Names from both the Bible and the Book of Mormon were often used: Manassa, Lehi, Moroni, Manti, Ephraim, and Nephi are but a few of the striking toponyms that the Mormons brought West with them. These names, along with names of powerful church leaders such as Joseph, Heber, and Brigham, give the visitor a sense of being in an area where religion is a dominant factor. An occasional roadside billboard may have a sober-looking Beneficial Life Insurance Company (Mormon-owned) theme; or on local highway signs one may encounter religious expressions such as, "Oh my people, shun evil in every form!" A somber uniformity can be sensed. The political conservatism ("Join the John Birch Society" one billboard proclaims) and religious fundamentalism of the region can almost be felt.

A huge white letter "C" is seen on the hill behind the group of trees and buildings that is Canaanville. This is the town's initial, erected by the school children. This big initial above such a small town seems peculiar: it is symbolic of the Mormon attitude which stresses education and keeps children busy. The huge letter, too, marks the town's pride: it is a statement of existence.

From afar the Mormon village appears as an island of buildings and trees in a sea of rectangular fields, cut into checkerboard patterns from semi-desert scrubland, and within sight of towering mountains or hills. The traveler gains access to Canaanville by traversing a sharp turn of the highway which flows into the town as "Main Street." This is the result of rigid N-S-E-W grid planning, and Main Street itself is a north-south broad-running corridor, almost 90 feet from curb to curb. A sign along the road informs the traveler: "Canaanville, pop. 508, elev. 5,121 ft."

Upon entering the town limits, the traveler has a lasting first impression: there is a myriad of buildings, fences and sheds, but none are really crowded together. In fact, the impression is almost one of a series of small farms pieced together to form a town. A rural feeling prevails because open pastures, barns, granaries, hay stacks, etc. are right in town (Fig. 3).

A conversation with any of the town's folk will reveal that Canaanville was not only settled and developed by the

Figure 3.—A Mormon Townscape: Fountain Green, Utah.

Mormons but that even today most of its 508 souls are Latter-day Saints. They are a friendly, yet reserved, folk. Their pace of life is slow, but they are almost always busy with church, house or farm work.

Canaanville once had a true village economy, and was virtually self-sufficient.[1] Agriculture was the mainstay. Each morning, stock were collectively driven out to the surrounding fields, and brought home in the evening. Today, however, individual farmers own stock which are grazed on the individually owned fields outside of town.

Since its inception in 1864, Canaanville had a fairly stable population, about 600. But since the 1930's and the depression that has changed. The town's agricultural economy is failing, and some farmers have left Canaanville for the city or areas where they could make a better living, such as Idaho. Thus, between 1930 and 1965 Canaanville lost almost 100 inhabitants. Abandoned homes can be spotted in the town, whose atmosphere is hardly prosperous, and which is even considered "dying" by some.

In the last few years, however, the town's citizens have noted with interest the arrival of three new families, all from California—people who have retired from the "ills of the city." Two of these families are "LDS," Latter-day Saints, or "Mormons." All have refurbished older homes. Along with virtually everyone else in the town, they enjoy the rural-town life characteristic of most Mormon villages. In Canaanville one can live on a farm right in town, thereby resolving the rural-urban dichotomy.[2] The village, as an early study noted, gives the impression

> . . . of an intensively cultivated and populous farm area. The peculiar manner in which the lots . . . had been cut detracted from rather than added to a town atmosphere.[3]

While the reference here is to Utah's Dixie, the description is applicable to Canaanville and most of the Mormon towns in the Intermontane West. In a few blocks farms give way to the small business district located on Main Street toward the center of town.

As the entire Mormon landscape involves the bold trinity of mountain, field and village, so the town itself can be divided by a visual trident; i.e., the public square, the business zone, and the residential farms. Canaanville is almost square in outline, about one half of a mile on each side, with commercial and religious life clustered toward the center (Fig. 4).

Very close to the center of town is the public square, a regular block, but open and park-like, upon which is located the LDS chapel and another, older church building, the Relief Society hall. Located on this same square is the schoolhouse, a substantial brick building built in 1898. All around the central square is the residential area itself, in reality a clustering of small farms.

Virtually all town business takes place in a small strip of commercial buildings along that wide, paved main street. The 88-foot-wide main street is lined only in a few places by trees—cottonwoods or locusts. Being a state highway, it is in good condition, but a glimpse down any side street reveals quite the opposite: Side streets have literally been scratched into the land's surface and are most often rutted and rilled. They, too, are wide, but since automobiles are driven down their centers only, the rest of the street is quite neglected. Canaanville's side streets are about 75 feet wide, but the roadway is effectively a twenty-foot strip in the center of two wide and weedy shoulders, each about 25 feet wide (Fig. 5). The shoulders are choked with sunflowers, milk weeds, purple, white and yellow clover, and some grasses. Canaanville's streets are ragged and overgrown, though some Mormon towns try to keep weeds and other plants down by scything and mowing. "We even mow our streets to keep our town clean, which is more than I can say for some other towns around here," a proud resident of Kanosh, Utah, told me. She could not realize how peculiar "mowing the streets" sounded, having spent all of her life in a Mormon town!

Actually, in Canaanville the road shoulders are used by the villagers for several important things. In fact, it might be proper to speak of "land use on the Mormon street." Stock

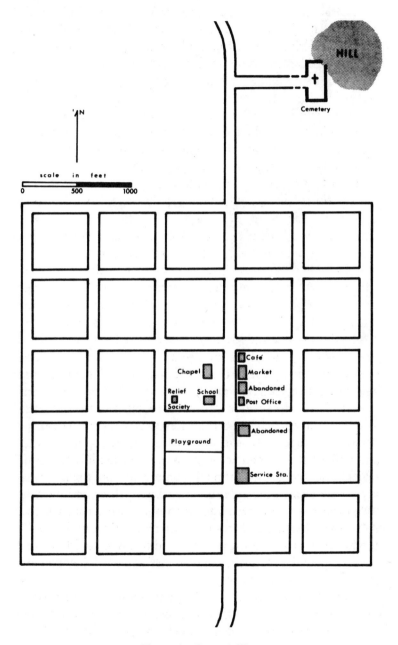

Figure 4.—Canaanville.

Figure 5.—A Wide Mormon Street at Spring City, Utah.

are often seen tethered to fence posts along the side of the road and allowed to graze out to the edge of the roadway part. Sometimes the mowed or scythed "crop" is brought to the stock in their corrals and used as feed. Parking is no problem with such wide roads, and agricultural equipment such as tractors and even larger equipment is often stored there until needed. Surely the shoulders would soon fail to be considered part of the street if it were not for the fact that Canaanville's city government still owns all of the legal road right-of-way up to a person's front yard, and insists that no private buildings be constructed on it. In some parts of Canaanville, barns will be seen bordering right on the street, but never infringing upon it.

The rutted dirt roads with their unruly sides and often weed-hidden ditches, as well as lack of sidewalks, are not conducive to walking. The family auto is extensively used instead, even for a trip of a block or two. Young children are seen walking, it is true, but many are seen riding their bicycles and horses along the roads.

Occasionally one can find the remnant of a narrow sidewalk, broken and weed-covered, running between fenced property line and ditch. This adds to the neglected, unruly aspect of the village. That sidewalk was probably once well-used before the turn of the century, but now pedestrians walk at the edge of the used road, forced into the street by parked equipment and grazing animals.

The roadside irrigation ditches are characteristic of virtually all Mormon villages, and are the lifelines of Canaanville. Much more than deep gutters, they are lines in an arterial system of water division which permit life as we see it in the village. While some towns in Canaan Valley have ditches lining the main street, in Canaanville these were replaced by underground pipe conduits during repaving, and cannot be detected due to the replacement of the regular curbing common throughout much of the United States.

But real ditches are still to be found along many side streets. While some are concrete-lined, most are just dug into the dirt roadside and are now weed- or grass-covered slots about 18 inches wide and 18 inches deep. Some are so overgrown with tall weeds that their presence can be detected only by the intense green color of vegetation along them and the almost constant murmur of flowing water. Some flow with less consistency, being fed by feeders higher up the line. The irrigation water is controlled by a series of "gates" which are inserted to divert water from one channel to another, quite often at right angles to it. The water then leaves its streetside location and enters the farmer's property, to be used for orchard, garden and pasture, all by a series of smaller gates devised by the farmer.

These gates, both at roadside and in the garden, are often merely a series of planks nailed together, inserted into slots in the canal or ditch. Sometimes they are pieces of sheet metal. Sometimes the water user makes do with anything he has; even discarded license plates have seen service along this line. But for larger ditches the newer guillotine-type head gate

Figure 6.—An Old Brick Home Seen
Through a Headgate, Monticello, Utah.

is often used (Fig. 6). It is a curious roadside element, a symbol vividly demonstrating that the entire town is dependent
for its very life on the irrigation water coursing down from
the mountains.

The omnipresent roadside ditch can be a source of delight
to youngsters as well as one of consternation to parents. A
child's fascination for running water is beautifully revealed
by the projects in which ambitious youngsters engage during
the hot summer days. On these lazy days, small boats of every
description come out of hiding and are launched in the muddy
waters of the ditch. The fun usually ends when larger toys,
such as bicycles, enter the canal for a maiden voyage (Fig. 7).

In Canaanville, the water user diverts his water strictly "by
turn" only—which may come during the night or day. The
farmer or gardener must be there to insert his gates to make
the proper diversion at the proper time. Otherwise he will lose
his turn, and his crops or pasture will suffer.

Figure 7.—Children Playing in a Roadside Ditch, Snowflake, Arizona.

If we liken these canals to major blood vessels, the aorta or real life line is the "big ditch" which runs through field and village. Even in town this canal is about three to eight feet wide and continually and rapidly flows to the fields across town. This large "stream," in contrast to the small roadside ditches, is a very real source of concern to those with small children. In some towns tragedies have occurred when small children have been swept away and drowned in the larger arterial canals.

Despite the problems they bring, the ditches symbolize man's conquest of a semi-arid region, and are delightful to see on a hot summer day. The sound of water and the sight of it splashing along is refreshing. In addition, Canaanville's dwellers are always aware of which direction is uphill, or downhill, and all variations in the contours of the land are made more obvious. While there is an old expression that "only the Mormons can make the water run uphill," the citizens of Canaanville can tell a visitor where the apex of an alluvial fan is because they have noted the direction in which water flows down the ditch. For even though roadsides are weedy, at each

intersection the water appears. It runs underground across
the intersection, but tends to form swirling, noisy pools at
the place where it enters the conduit for its brief trip under a
crossing street.

Not only Canaanville's spacious streets, with their weedy
shoulders and irrigation ditches, but the blocks themselves
are also large—30 rods square—and land use on them right
up to the city center has a spacious, rural quality rarely encountered in non-Mormon towns.

Each of Canaanville's large blocks is squarely divided up
into four lots, though a few blocks closer to the town center
have been divided up into six lots, a result of more recent
"subdivision." Most blocks, however, contain the originally
surveyed four lots. On the typical block divided into fours,
there is a house on each corner lot, the house set back about
30 feet from the corner. The interior portion of the lot is a
rectangular maze of corrals, gardens, pasture-land, barn and
shed-like buildings, granaries and outhouses (Fig. 8). Everything adheres strictly to the N-S-E-W grid. All buildings line
up with the compass.

The wide spacing of homes on a block, with a cluster of
four at a street corner, is typically "Mormon." It has been
noted that "the houses, instead of being located near the
middle of the plots, are grouped in fours at the street intersec-
tions . . ."[4] This is perhaps the most sociable arrangement
possible. Such wide streets and large lots would otherwise
tend to separate homes by great distances.

Not only house orientation, but certain house types seen
in Canaanville are unusual. Indeed, architecture is one of the
important diagnostic properties of Mormon towns, and Canaanville is no exception. Often seen is the central-hall plan
house type, which is rare to non-existent in most non-Mormon
towns in the Intermontane region. In Canaanville, these are
called "Nauvoo style houses."

Characterized by symmetrical plans and facades, one and a
half to two stories in height, and, most importantly, with a
chimney at each end, this is one of the most substantial house
types built in the West. The central-hall plan house, a general

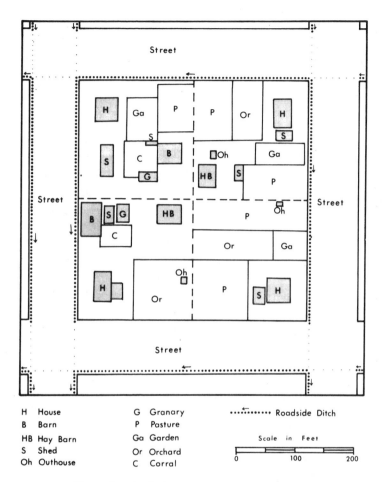

H	House	G	Granary	···←········ Roadside Ditch
B	Barn	P	Pasture	
HB	Hay Barn	Ga	Garden	Scale in Feet
S	Shed	Or	Orchard	
Oh	Outhouse	C	Corral	0 100 200

Figure 8.—Typical Farm Block in Canaanville.

type based on symmetrical floor plan, includes both the narrow, one room deep "I-style" and the wider "four over four" styles as sub-types. The home lends an Old-World—almost English—appearance to the village, especially when its small peaked dormer gables interrupt the roof line. On some, the two doors seen on the facade often are called "polygamy doors," and these have been commented on by visitors for a long time. Usually this type of house will have cornices of the Greek revival mode, which tend even more to create a heavy roof line and gable. This, coupled with the fact that the central-hall plan type was often built in brick (either adobe or fired) and stone, tends to make the house a very sturdy, almost fortress-like, element in the landscape (Figs. 9 and 10). About one third of the homes in Canaanville are of this type or some minor modification of it.

The "T-" and "L-" plan houses so often seen in Canaanville are elaborations on the central-hall plan, but often possess other elements which make them unique in appearance. Taller chimneys more characteristic of the Victorian era are one element, as is a more complete pediment in the Greek manner.

Figure 9.—An Adobe Central-Hall House Type, Nephi, Utah.

Figure 10.—A Brick Central-Hall Plan House
in a Typical Mormon Setting, Wales, Utah.

Often the upper part of the brick gable end will be rendered
in shingle, thus creating a contrast and breaking the simple
solid gable. Again, brick is a common material for this type
of house, which accounts for about one-fourth of Canaanville's homes.

   Houses exhibiting a more Victorian heritage can be found
in Canaanville, but they are not common. Most were built
around 1900 and are characterized by bay windows, steeply
pitched or hipped roofs, ornate cornices, complex asymmet-
rical floor plans, elaborate porches and sometimes even cu-
polas. Only a few houses in the town are of this type. Most
were owned by wealthier families. Some are brick, some wood.
Whatever the materials, they tend to overshadow the simpler
homes nearby.

   Other, smaller houses are seen in Canaanville. The bunga-
low is so called because it has a large porch, the roof line being
continued out over the porch rather than the latter being a

mere addition. It is a low solid structure, rather than having a steep roof. The roof is most often hipped, though simple pitched gable roofs occur too.

There are two other types of houses seen in Canaanville, one with simple gable roofs, and the other with hipped roofs. They are almost nondescript in their simplicity. Both are of varying floor plans, but generally have their main fireplace toward the center of the home. Chimneys are seen at or near the center of the house (Fig. 11). There is nothing "Mormon" about these houses; the traveler can see them almost everywhere in the West. Yet the fact that they are often built in brick, with depressed arches above the windows and doors, and are interspersed with the solid, more substantial rectangular, T-, and L-plan types makes them important. A variety of domestic architecture, and visual but not usually numerical dominance of substantial structures, typifies Canaanville and is characteristic of most Mormon towns.

Figure 11.—Brick Version of a Simple Gable Roof House at Paragonah, Utah.

Of the other half dozen or so homes built since the Second World War, most are of the so-called "ranch style." Again, these houses cannot be called Mormon at all, but there are some elements which reflect LDS traditions in building. Sometimes the most modern ranch-style house will sport a weighty Greek-Revival pediment reminiscent of the central-hall houses. Architecturally, Canaanville is made up of consistently-chosen building types. The building materials, too, are likely to impress the traveler. Fully forty percent of Canaanville's houses are built of a "salmon pink" to darker red-colored brick; a few, five percent, are of stone. Many others, about thirty percent, are stuccoed over so that it is impossible to tell their original material. Only about twenty-five percent of the houses are obviously frame dwellings. The feeling is one of a durable architecture, never overly ornate. Any decorative detail is an integral part of the structures such as eaves and arches. Elaborate carving is rare, and appears to have been added to originally plain houses. The architectural complexion of the town is pre-Victorian.

Around most of Canaanville's substantial homes are trees of various types. Locusts, fruit trees, maples and poplars were commonly planted near the older homes. The newer homes have some young trees near them, but bushes are now becoming popular. This is no doubt part of a general trend in modern American landscape architecture, with smaller, more spreading plants to harmonize with the lines of the "ranch style."

The house, whether built of brick, stone or wood, is often a symmetrical and solid unit, well maintained, though there are important exceptions. Barns and other farm buildings, which stand behind the homes, are quite another story.

Barns are an important part of the townscape of Canaanville, as distinct from the typical non-Mormon town. Wherever the Mormon village pattern was established, barns were an integral part of it. The barn type which is characteristic of Mormon farms is a rectangular building with a simple pitched roof and often an adjoining shed on one or both sides. The early ones were often made with the lower portion in notched log construction. This was apparently common

Figure 12.—An Old Log-Style Barn, Spring City, Utah.

in the early days, for the two oldest barns are of this type (Fig. 12). Some barns standing in Canaanville are the originals, put up in the 1860's.

Newer barns are generally of the same type, but made of all wood planks, running vertically (Fig. 13). The same general conditions of maintenance prevail. Often the shingles are partly gone from the roof, planks are missing from the siding, and some lean at precarious angles.

The "hay barn" is a framed, open-sided structure often with partial sides of log, plank or boards (Fig. 14). These are used for storing hay, and usually have an extended ridge pole serving as a lift to the hayloft above. They are the most dilapidated buildings in the farmyard scene. Sometimes they are empty, sometimes full of hay. Almost always they are leaning at a slight angle. Some which lean much further seem to be propped up by the hay in the barn and little else.

The finish of a Mormon barn is unpainted, and has been burnished to a silvered or brownish sheen by years of weathering under the fierce summer sun and icy winter gales. The local

Figure 13.—An Old Plank-Sided Barn, Levan, Utah.

Figure 14.—Hay Barn, Spring City, Utah.

Mormons in Canaanville even have stories and jokes about the condition of their farm buildings. One farmer was once asked by a visitor if it was "a Mormon superstition" not to repair and paint barns, to which he replied, "Heck no, we're just too busy to fool around with that sort of thing."

Granaries, too, are weathered structures which have never seen a paint brush. Some of the older ones are solid and made of stone. But, most often, one sees what the American geographer-folklorist Henry Glassie has called the "inside-out" granary. The vertical studding is on the outside, the clapboarding is on the inside, and forms, therefore, a smooth interior. Grain is stored in these structures, which are divided into several bins for different varieties. These are a distinctive element in the Mormon landscape. Their construction technique gives them the appearance of being unfinished, but their weathered surfaces tell the visitor they have been there for a long time (Fig. 15).

Figure 15.—An "Inside-Out" Granary at Spring City, Utah.

The small sheds for animals resemble those small stick-like shelters, or "ramadas," constructed by the Navajo Indians in northern Arizona. Frequently, the roof on these small sheds will be either loose or baled hay—a "thatched" roof of sorts (Fig. 16). These, too, are often leaning at angles, but they still serve the purpose of keeping stock and equipment out of the weather.

Around these small sheds, and also partly surrounding the barn, is the corral, a place where stock is kept and fed. The fences used are often the pole and runner style, and sometimes what is called the "Mormon fence"—a strange picket fence made of various types of poles, slabs, posts, and even regular pickets, all unpainted (Fig. 17). The bleached, grayish-whitish wood of these corrals forms a distinct contrast to the dark brown earth and manure in the corral itself.

The "hay derrick" is another unpainted stick-like element in the landscape which serves to give the barnyard a primitive, rustic character. Several main types are to be seen. They all

Figure 16.—Typical Mormon Village Scene, Beaver, Utah.

work on the same fulcrum-pulley principle. When several are seen together, the effect is one of masts and booms, lending a ship-yard or port atmosphere to the landscape.

Often the hay derrick is no longer in use. Nevertheless, there it will remain—in the barnyard—many times decapitated from its base, or lacking a pulley, its rotting rope swinging through the winds and breezes of countless seasons. "I just don't have the time to take it down. Besides, I may be able to use something from it," was one explanation. Actually many hay derricks are still in operation in Canaanville and other parts of the Mormon West, though most people will say, "We don't use 'em anymore."

The hay pile is an ever-present part of the barnyard. While some hay is stored in hay barns, much of it is left out in large rectangular stacks composed of bales. These golden-to-greenish bales are stacked either with a hay derrick (using a Jackson fork), by hand, or by a mechanical hay loader. Along with a

Figure 17.—A Mormon Fence, Bunkerville, Nevada.

fantastic collection of old, used, rusting parts from automobiles, tractors, and other equipment, as well as old wagon parts, and piles of wood to be used both for firewood and in making patchwork repairs, they form the curious collection that is the farmyard. Even old automobiles may be kept nearby in hope that some part may be useful in future days.

Also located amid this clutter on some lots is the old outhouse (called a "back house" in Canaanville). Since all houses now have bathrooms, these are remnants of the earlier days. Usually leaning at a slight angle, and located near a property line, the small unpainted outhouses with their little "windows" are a characteristic element in the Mormon landscape (Fig. 18). They are regarded with mingled disdain and affection by the village folk.

The vegetable garden is an important part of the Mormon landscape. The typical Mormon family depends on it for much of its vegetable food supply. Usually the garden will be located to one side of the house on its corner lot, relatively close to the house. Maize is an important crop, though most villagers

Figure 18.—An Outhouse at Spring City, Utah.

try to raise all of the types of crops they will need throughout the remainder of the year. Carrots, peas, beans, tomatoes, squash, melons are all grown, and are canned or stored for the winter in substantial earthen or block cellars beneath their homes, or in modern freezers. The average Mormon is proud of his garden and conversation in the village often runs along the lines of how someone's crop is doing.

This is especially true of flower gardens. The flower garden is the real pride and joy of many families in Canaanville. Roses and gladiolas are the main types raised, though a host of other types are also grown. The bright patches of color in an otherwise rather drab unpainted landscape are impressive. Young adults in Canaanville, however, are finding less and less time and enthusiasm for flower growing, and a fine garden usually demarcates an older person's home.

Some farmers have small orchards in their large yards. These are mostly of peach, apple, apricot, and cherry trees. The orchard close to the home, often neglected, scrubby and weedy, is a typical element in the landscape of Canaanville. Sheep and cattle are seen grazing on the grass beneath the neglected trees.

The typical Mormon lot also has a pasture on which a few cattle, horses and sheep are grazed. This patch of green—contrasting with the brown of the barnyard and the grayish-brown of the farm buildings—is usually located farthest away from the house, either toward the center of the block, or along the street side about half way down the block.

All this diverse land use in one lot, on one "city" block, calls for a good deal of fencing to keep activities separate (to keep grazing animals out of the garden, for instance). The typical Mormon lot thus requires many linear feet of fence; but fence is expensive, and materials on hand must suffice for much of the fencing.

At one time the rip-gut fence was to be seen in Canaanville. This was a crude fence composed of cedar twigs and branches stuck in the ground and placed in "cross" fashion against each other. It was one more unpainted, crooked element in an already cluttered landscape.

Since old poles, planks and boards are kept, they can be put to use here. The Mormon fence is not only used for the corral. Often it is used for much of the lot, even near the home. Besides starting out relatively crooked because cedar and juniper are frequently-used woods, they are patched with the most ill-fitting, rustic-looking boards, and the fence becomes an unpainted potpourri of different types and shapes of wood. There appears to be little concern for, or awareness of, beauty when fences are considered. In one fence one may count as many as five different picket styles, from simple two-by-fours to an ornate Victorian picket once used around the house itself. An old wagon wheel or hay rake may be seen forming part of a fence somewhere in Canaanville.

Thus an important part of the rustic, rural feeling of the Mormon village is a result of the farmyard settings right in town. The large and solid houses; the barns and granaries; the hay derricks, gardens, orchards, and sheds all conspire to bring the farm right to city center.

The center or business district of the town is a strip-like development with businesses stretching along the wide, paved, main street. It is composed of a cafe, grocery store, post office, service station and two abandoned buildings. While there is nothing especially "Mormon" about this business strip, unless it is the lack of a bar, the fact that Canaanville's businesses are within sight of barns and pastures is typically Mormon. Downtown on the main street, in front of the post office, there is a continually running fountain, a refreshing and unique fixture in a semi-arid region.

The center of community life in the town, however, is not the business district, but the LDS ward chapel which serves as a meeting house, dance hall, gathering place, meeting place for the women's Relief Society, and a place for patriotic and other gatherings (Fig. 19).

As was noted, the church is located on what is still referred to as the "square" or "public square." Virtually all LDS towns were laid out with reference to a square which was located in the center of town. On this the church, school, park and other religious buildings such as Welfare and Relief Society buildings

Figure 19.—The Mormon Chapel as seen from the
General Store, Kanosh, Utah.

were located. Even today this is the secular and religious focal
point of town.

The Canaanville LDS ward chapel has a distinctive architectural character which may be seen throughout Mormon
country. It is a low brick building crowned by a steeple, and
with Georgian decorative detail. Built in 1951, it is strangely
devoid of any religious symbolism such as the cross. Painfully
small, neat letters in dark metal stretch across its facade:
Church of Jesus Christ of Latter-day Saints. The ward chapel's
long wings give the impression of a school building. It has a
character that is at once religious and public-institutional.

Because the chapel is a large building, rambling far and
topped by a steeple, and because the townscape is open and
rural, the LDS church can be seen from several blocks away
while its spire often crowns the rustic scene—a juxtaposition

at once striking and also symbolic of the omnipresence of the Church in the life of the village.

The dominance of the LDS church in the spiritual and cultural lives of the village-folk can be discerned from other clues, such as the lack of churches of other denominations, and the absence of Masonic halls or buildings of other secret orders (membership in which is actively discouraged by the Church).

Ironically, Canaanville school is also indicative of the power of the LDS church in the community. The school is more representative of Victorian institutional architecture than anything "Mormon" (Fig. 20). And yet its location on the same property as the only church in the town is significant, and speaks of a fusion of church and state that was once a way of life in Deseret. The visual juxtaposition of church and school still serves as a constant reminder of the dominance of religion in the lives of Canaanville's citizens.

Canaanville's ward chapel now serves numerous religious and social functions, but many years ago each function was

Figure 20.—The Public School, Kanosh, Utah.

carried on in a separate building. As noted, the public square possessed several small structures such as a Relief Society hall, Tithing office, amusement halls, and so on.

Each small structure was built substantially, usually of brick or stone. While style varied, the Greek Revival was the most dominant. All that is left of these old buildings in Canaanville is the stone Relief Society hall (Fig. 21). The solid cornices of the interrupted Greek pediment grace this building, too. The fate of the Relief Society hall is uncertain; it may be demolished soon, or saved by groups interested in local history. The old church buildings, of course, never had a counterpart in non-Mormon towns. Even today the old Relief Society hall is an important element in the townscape of Canaanville.

Some years ago, before they were demolished, pure LDS visual symbolism could be seen on certain of those church buildings. The earlier ward chapel, and small endowment hall were especially rich in symbols, such as the Beehive ("Industry;" the Mormon state of Deseret meant "honeybee"), the square and the compass, and other "Liberty and Virtue" symbols reminiscent of the Masonic Order (Fig. 22). Stars signifying the Celestial Kingdom also appeared. Today such symbols are becoming rare as exterior ornamentation, the circle within a ring atop the chapel steeple ("eternity") being a subtle exception.

Not only in life, but in the rites of death too, Canaanville can be distinguished from Gentile communities. Its cemetery differs from one which might be found in a non-Mormon town: though the basic forms of its tombstones appear similar to non-Mormon ones, with Gothic arch style stones, obelisks, and tablets appearing, the "Book of Mormon," "L" and "V" symbols, stars, and other images such as the temple at Salt Lake City, can be found on some stones, albeit a minority of them.

Another peculiarity of the Canaanville cemetery is the appearance of small "footstones" in addition to the regular headstones. These footstones mark the end of the plot, and frequently have the initials of the deceased on them. They

Figure 21.—Old Relief Society Hall, Escalante, Utah.

Figure 22.—Classic Mormon Symbolism on the Endowment Hall at Spring City, Utah.

characterize the older graves, and are usually made out of the same material as the head stones. Newer graves do not have these markers, and are usually characterized by the typical modern markers which are almost flush with the ground.

IMPRESSIONS OF MORMON COUNTRY

Canaanville is therefore a town very different, both culturally and visually, from a non-Mormon town. Certain elements are likely to leave vivid, lasting impressions on the traveler: a view down a weedgrown irrigation ditch and an old Mormon fence along side a wide roadway, toward solid brick homes— one on each street corner; tall poplars in lines or in clumps, several of which are dead or dying; gray or brownish barns, sagging with broken ridge poles; hay barns, mere skeletons of poles and posts raising their spindly forms in the already dilapidated barnyard; domestic architecture with an Old-World or perhaps archaic eastern United States character placed against the bold sage- and cedar-covered mountains and hills of the mountain West: these are impressions of Canaanville, and of Mormon country.

Not only forms and their combinations, but colors too leave lasting impressions. The intense lemonish and lime greens of haying lands, the resplendent dark olive greens of poplars, are striking in a buff or grayish-green setting of rock and sage. Clear light floods the scene, bringing to full intensity even the most pastel of hues. The gray and silver hues of barns and other outbuildings contrast vividly with the flat buffs and reds of solid homes. There is a geography of color related to Mormon settlement, just as there is a geography of specific forms or elements.[5] Impressions of Canaanville are indeed striking, and involve a totality of visual experience.

Canaanville and its environs form a visual entity which is repeated throughout Mormon country, not dozens, but hundreds of times. Many travelers have reported being bored to distraction while traveling through Mormon country and its towns which have such a singularly similar and rural appearance. Mr. Golden Oldroyd, a motel owner in Nephi, Utah, likes to tell the story about the young man who traveled through Utah on his way from California to New York, and stopped that night in Nephi and called his father in New York. "Dad," he said, "you surely wouldn't like Utah, just one little town just like the next, set up by the Kingfish for each wife." He was apparently referring to the popular (if erroneous) image of Brigham Young and the polygamy situation in years past. "But Dad," he then added, "you'd sure like Las Vegas!" (Interestingly, Las Vegas itself was originally founded by the Mormons. The early settlers, however, were recalled to Salt Lake City by Church leaders, and the community developed first as a railroad town, later into a gambling center.)

Mr. Oldroyd's anecdote, on the grossest level, reflects an awareness that Mormon settlements are generally rather uniform and different from Gentile settlements, and also that not all of the West is dominated by the Mormons. It is with this in mind that we shall consider the next topic: how unique are the elements in Canaanville; how specifically related to the Mormons are they; and how are they distributed across the face of the Intermontane West?

NOTES

1. See L. J. Arrington, *Great Basin Kingdom: Economic History of the Latter-Day Saints, 1830-1900* (Lincoln: University of Nebraska Press, 1958); and Albert L. Seeman, "Communities in the Salt Lake Basin," *Economic Geography*, Vol. 14 (1938), pp. 300-308, for a discussion of the economic characteristics of Utah settlements.
2. H. C. Smith, "City Planning," *Journal of History*, Vol. 15 (1922), pp. 1-17, contains perceptive comments on the Mormon village pattern and the rural-urban preferences of Americans.

3. J. E. Spencer, "The Middle Virgin River Valley, Utah: A Study in Culture Growth and Change" (unpublished Ph.D. dissertation, University of California, Berkeley, 1936), p. 120.

4. J. W. Reps, *Town Planning in Frontier America* (Princeton: Princeton University Press, 1969), p. 419.

5. For a discussion of this often neglected subject, see E. T. Price, "A Geography of Color," *Geographical Review*, Vol. 54 (1964), pp. 590-592.

CHAPTER 2

The Mormon Landscape Through Space and Time

Canaanville, and its environs, is a generalization based on impressions of Mormon country. As no two towns anywhere are identical, however, it must be remembered that two Mormon towns separated by almost 1,000 miles of rugged, semi-arid country are bound to have some differences.

The questions at hand are traditionally geographical ones. How are the cultural elements observed at Canaanville distributed in space? Where are these found in the West? And, using the Mormon elements, does there arise a spatially definable entity called "Mormon Country?"

SOME METHODS

With the exception of chapel architecture, certain tombstones and the smaller secondary religious structures located on the public squares, none of the elements discussed at Canaanville are restricted totally to the Mormons. An example: The Lombardy poplar can be seen near Gentile settlements as well as Mormon. This is true, to a lesser extent, of the "hay derrick." But landscape is not a series of isolated elements, even though individual entities can be very important. Rather, landscape involves the presence and visual combination of a

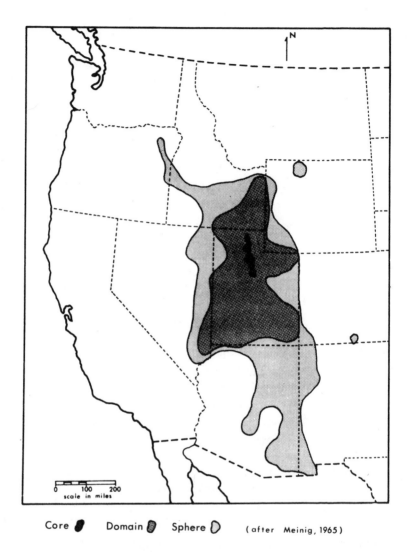

Core 🌑   Domain 🌑   Sphere 🌘   (after   Meinig, 1965)

Figure 38.—The Western United States: Hay Derricks.

series of elements which together compose a scene or compage, in this case a Mormon scene.

But a look at the distribution of individual elements will be of value in giving spatial bounds to Mormon country. Only by a careful analysis of these can we understand which are pan-Mormon, which are partially Mormon, and which are non-Mormon. In the proper combinations, both in quantity and quality, these elements become landscape.

While virtually all of Mormon country was visited and studied (and compared to a large portion of the surrounding non-Mormon area), a sample of 42 towns was chosen which would represent Mormon, partially Mormon and non-Mormon places. The framework used was Meinig's "Mormon Culture Region" (Fig. 23), and towns were chosen which were thought to represent most of the Intermontane and Mountain West. Population was restricted to towns from 300 to 2,000, and, to keep variables as nearly controlled as possible, all towns had economies based (past or present) at least in part on farming rather than mining, recreation, or other forms of livelihood. It would be unfair to compare a Mormon farming village to a western mining town, because even the most casual travelers note differences between these. The towns selected are shown on Fig. 24.

Nor was the study limited to just these 42 towns. A count of various elements was made for several hundred small towns, and these elements appear in abstracted form in a map entitled "Visual Characteristics of Mormon Country (p. 72)." In addition, notes and descriptions of virtually all of the area under consideration were taken; these helped in compiling the final map.

Meinig's main area is a fairly accurate concept. Within the core, however, heavy urbanization has either veneered, disguised or obliterated much of the rural landscape. Within the domain are found many real Mormon farming villages developed on the classic pattern. And in the sphere of Meinig's region lie both Mormon and non-Mormon settlements. In this surrounding sphere area two main patterns dominate: 1) true

Figure 24.—Selected Towns in the Western United States.

Mormon villages, founded in the later 1800's, most of which are still Mormon in population today (e.g., Snowflake, Arizona); 2) a more dispersed settlement of more recent times (e.g., the Mormon populations along the Snake River Plain) dating from the first half of the present century. Hagerman, Idaho, is a good example of an area settled since the turn of the century by the Mormons. Gentiles still dominate in many of these areas.

As a rule, a "Mormon town" is one that was either settled exclusively by the Mormons, usually before 1900, or one in which the Mormons dominate numerically today—in numbers over 75%. The latter is, however, rare (McCammon, Idaho, once a railroad town, is mostly LDS today). For the most part the "Mormon towns" in the West were settled by Mormon pioneers. Some of these even today are almost 100% LDS in population.

Fig. 25 shows towns which fit the descriptions Mormon (ca. 75+% LDS), partly Mormon (35-75% LDS), and non-Mormon (less than 20% LDS). Keeping these towns in mind, we shall now investigate how they relate to the occurence of various landscape elements, such as poplars, hay derricks, etc. and the frames of reference within which they occur.

ELEMENTS IN SPACE

As a framework for many elements, the rigid North-South-East-West grid system is of course important in Mormon country. It is to be noted, however, that there is nothing especially Mormon about it (Fig. 26). Non-Mormon towns are usually platted on the same system.

Wide streets, on the other hand, are more frequently encountered in Mormon towns (Fig. 27). If we use 65 feet as the dividing line between narrow and wide, Mormon towns stand out. Streets of over 80 feet are, in fact, to be seen in Mormon towns only, although many Mormon towns do have narrower streets. Street width of over 100 feet as seen in some

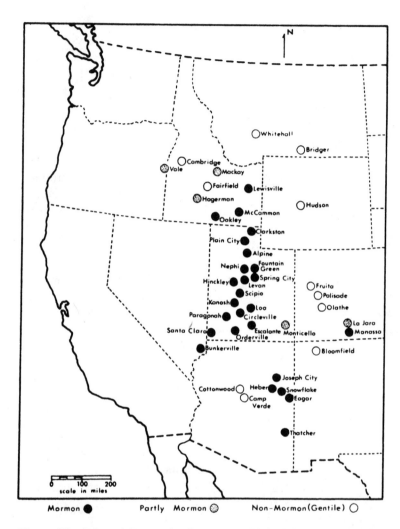

Figure 25.—Selected Towns in the Western United States: Population Characteristics.

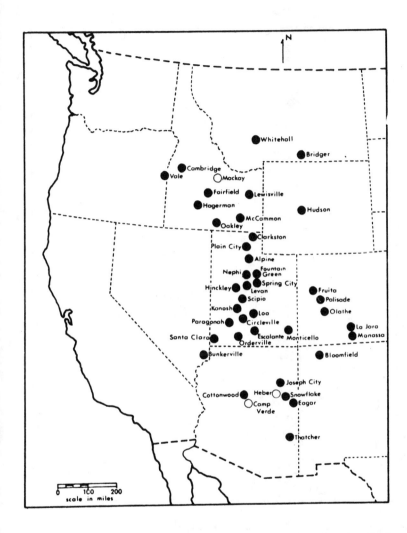

Figure 26.—Selected Towns in the Western United States: N-S-E-W Grid Plan.

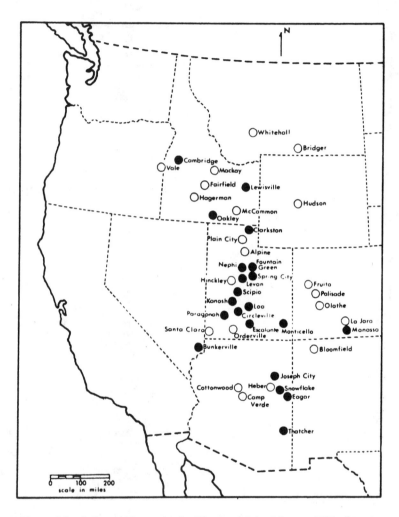

Figure 27.—Selected Towns in the Western United States: Wide Streets.

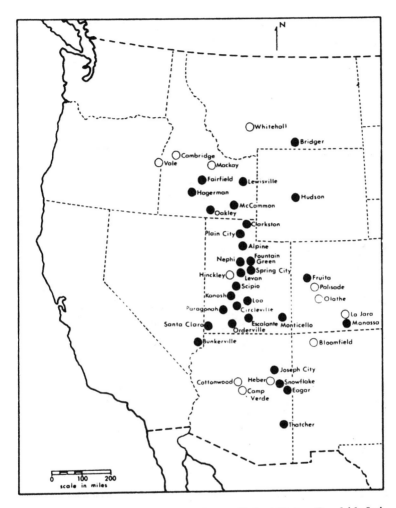

Figure 28.—Selected Towns in the Western United States: Roadside Irrigation Ditches.

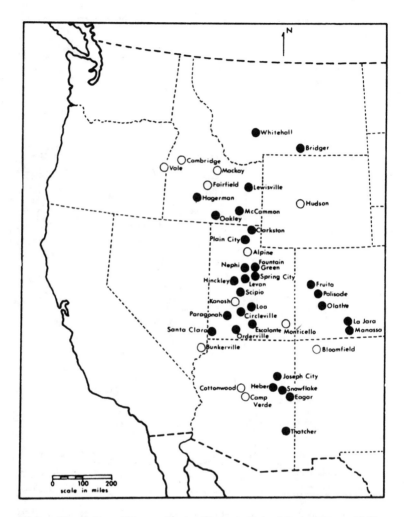

Figure 29.—Selected Towns in the Western United States: Trees Lining Streets.

Mormon towns (e.g., Kanosh, Utah) is unparalleled in the non-Mormon West. Lining these streets one often sees irrigation ditches, as was noted in Canaanville. Most Mormon towns studied had these, as do some non-Mormon towns (Fig. 28). In Mormon towns, however, these ditches are often deeper and wider than their Gentile counterparts, and are more often diverted by gates to gardens, pastures and orchards. Although one sees ditches in non-Mormon towns, they more often resemble deep gutters than the functional Mormon ditches.

The streets are often lined with trees in Mormon towns, as they are in non-Mormon towns (Fig. 29). While Mormon towns might have a slightly greater tendency to have tree-lined streets, this can hardly be considered Mormon at all. That Mormon towns today have more trees than non-Mormon appears to be a myth often repeated in Mormon country.

The town as it relates to the surrounding countryside is of course important. Open fields devoid (or nearly so) of buildings or farmsteads appear to be closely associated with many Mormon towns, while no non-Mormon towns have this characteristic (Fig. 30).

Sheep and cattle grazing on the same pasture is a trait which seems to bear some correlation with the Mormons (Fig. 31), although other people occasionally practice it. There seems to be a greater tendency to integrate stock among the older Mormon farmers.

The appearance of the Lombardy poplar (Fig. 32) is noted both in purely Mormon communities and in much of the non-Mormon West, too—e.g., Colorado, Arizona, Idaho, and Eastern Oregon. Importantly, however, most Mormon communities have poplars in nearby fields or even as part of the townscape. The poplar, like so many other "Mormon" elements, is not purely Mormon, but is merely highly represented in Mormon country. Nevertheless, it forms an important part of the visual impact. The poplar is the dominant tree only in certain areas, such as central Utah (near Glenwood) and in

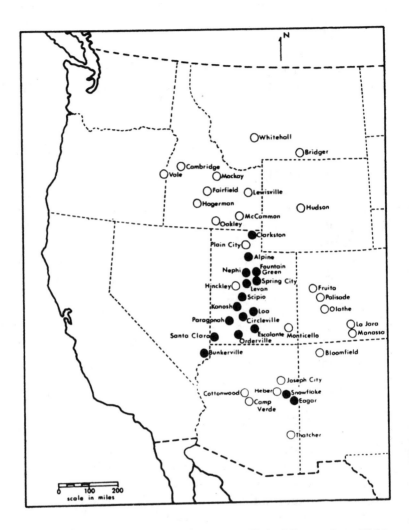

Figure 30.—Selected Towns in the Western United States: Open Fields Surrounding Town.

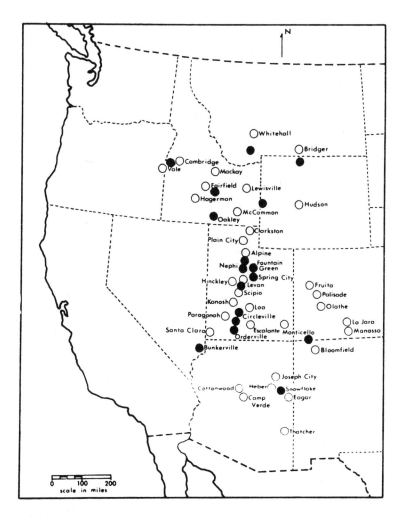

Figure 31.—Selected Towns in the Western United States: Cattle & Sheep on Same Pasture.

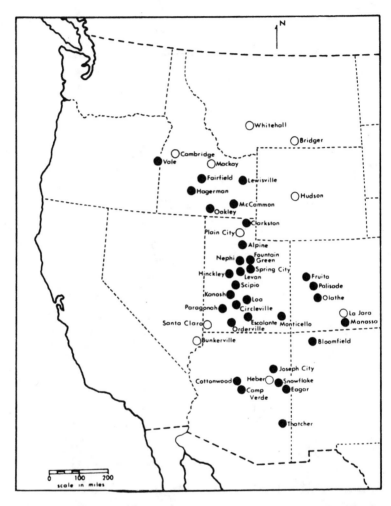

Figure 32.—Selected Towns in the Western United States: Lombardy Poplars in the Landscape.

the Snake River Plain. In other areas it appears, but with less impact; indeed, many poplars are dying and are not being replaced.

One of the most significant characteristics of Mormon villages is the appearance of "farm settings" right in town. As noted, corrals and pasturelands with grazing animals in town (Fig. 33) are restricted to most, but not all, of the Mormon towns studied.

The presence of barns and granaries right in town is also Mormon (Fig. 34). Most of these are not painted. Unpainted farm structures are definitely associated with the Mormons (Fig. 35). All of this serves to bring the farm into the village only in Mormon towns. Non-Mormon towns are usually devoid of farm buildings.

The only non-Mormon town seen with the "rural look" of a Mormon village was Greeley, Colorado. In this case, the influence is directly traceable to Mormon concepts of planning which the leaders of the Union Colony at Greeley sought to emulate.[1]

Specific elements are of great importance in this rural setting. The "inside-out" granary (Fig. 36) is seen throughout much of Mormon country. The "Mormon fence" (Fig. 37) is another frequent element, as is the hay derrick (Fig. 38), which is closely associated with the Mormons, especially in the central, northern and northwestern areas. Alfalfa haying is a dominant occupation in these areas. Toward the south, in Arizona, haying is of minor importance. The correlation between these derricks and the Mormons is certainly not one-to-one; in some areas non-Mormons own and use many of them. Nevertheless, there is a suspiciously close correlation, and in many areas they are called "Mormon hay derricks" or "Mormon stackers."

It has been noted that "Mormon architecture" is unique. The central-hall house, for example, is closely associated with the Mormons (Fig. 39). While not totally restricted only to Mormon communities (e.g., some may be seen in Jacksonville, Oregon), their presence in large numbers in a town implies

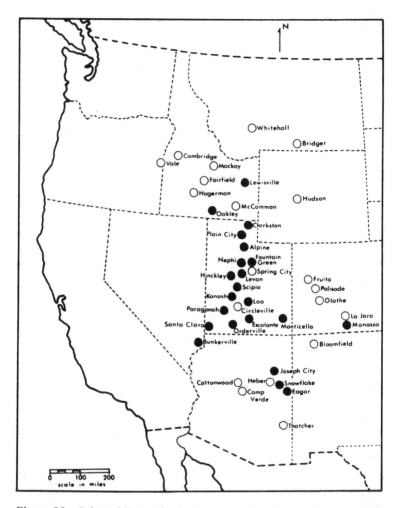

Figure 33.—Selected Towns in the Western United States: Farm Settings in Town.

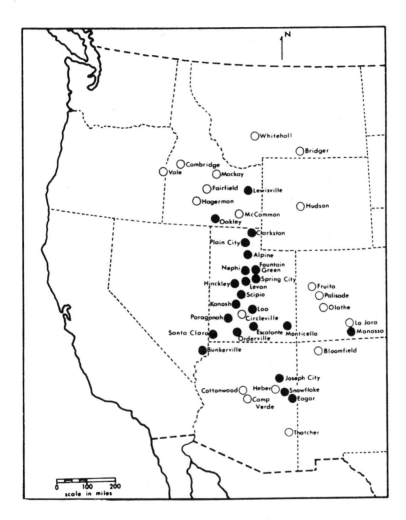

Figure 34.—Selected Towns in the Western United States: Barns & Granaries.

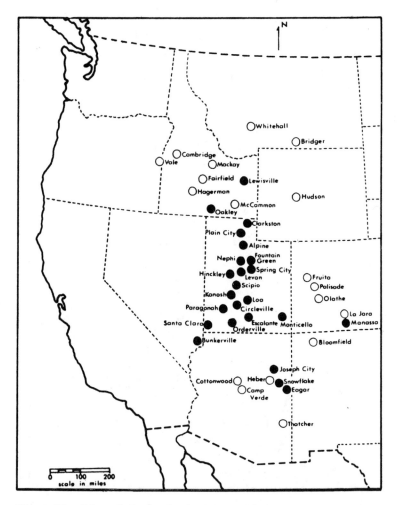

Figure 35.—Selected Towns in the Western United States: Unpainted
Farm Buildings.

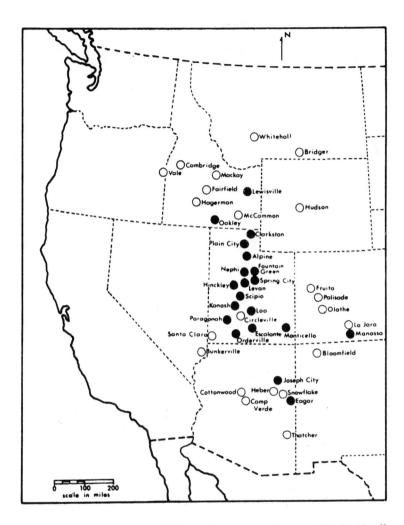

Figure 36.—Selected Towns in the Western United States: "Inside-Out"
Granaries.

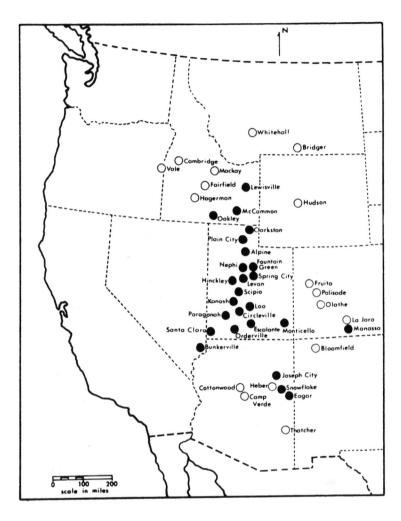

Figure 37.—Selected Towns in the Western United States: Mormon Fences.

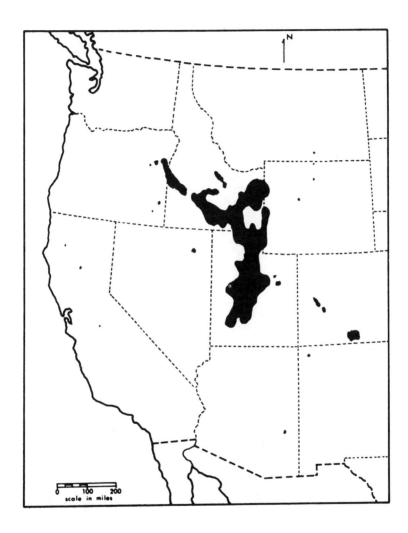

Figure 38.—The Western United States: Hay Derricks.

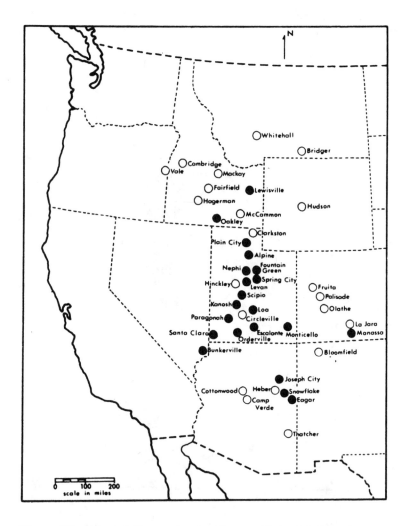

Figure 39.—Selected Towns in the Western United States: Central-Hall Plan Houses.

Mormon settlement when seen west of the Missouri River.[2] T-
and L-plan types of houses appear in both Mormon and non-
Mormon towns, as do ranch-style houses, bungalows, and
others. A high percentage of these structures in brick, e.g., more
than 30%, suggests a Mormon town. And any town with over
50% of its homes built of brick in this part of the West will
almost certainly be a Mormon town (Fig. 40). Towns like
Oakley, Idaho; Snowflake, Arizona; Fountain Green and Pan-
guitch, Utah, are classic examples. The latter, while not a town
studied in detail, has about 70% of its homes built of brick.
As a rule, one does not encounter such high figures except in
Ohio and many parts of the East. The West, usually, is an area
of wooden framed or stucco plaster homes. Only in Mormon
country does that substantial, eastern or middle western quality return in earnest. While some Mormon towns are low in
their percentage of brick houses (e.g., Manassa, Colorado, and
Eagar, Arizona), most rate higher than non-Mormon towns.

Another important part of the landscape is the color of
the homes in these towns. Mormon towns tend to have a
higher percentage of "warm" tones, especially red and light
brown (beige). Fig. 41 shows that much of Mormon country
has this appearance. While a few LDS towns lack this, only
one non-Mormon town qualifies (Cambridge, Idaho). With a
very few exceptions, in addition, Gentile towns tend to have
a higher percentage of white houses (Fig. 42). Mormon architecture, including the wooden buildings, features an earthen
color.

Mormon architecture, too, tends to lag behind non-Mormon by several years. Upon inquiry, one learns that the pre-
tentious Victorian homes occasionally seen were often built
twenty or more years later than similar styles in Gentile towns.
For example, there is a Victorian villa house in Moroni, Utah,
built in 1898. Similar styles were employed in the non-Mormon West in the 1870's and early 1880's. Naturally, all of
these factors tend to set Mormon architecture apart from non-
Mormon. The difference between Colorado and Utah towns

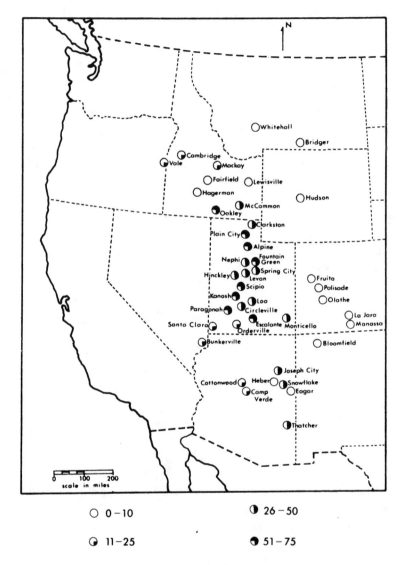

Figure 40.—Selected Towns in the Western United States: Percentage of Brick Houses.

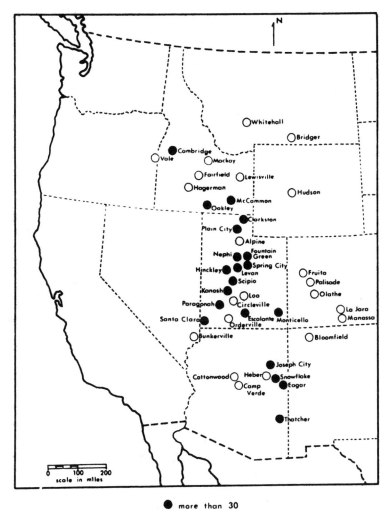

Figure 41.—Selected Towns in the Western United States: Percentage of Red & Light Brown Houses.

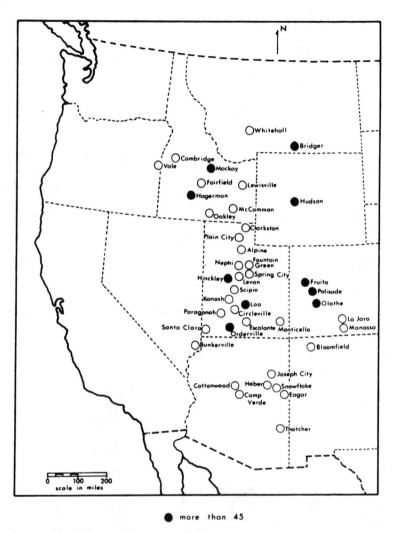

Figure 42.—Selected Towns in the Western United States: Percentage of White Houses.

THROUGH SPACE AND TIME   63

is striking. Even Mormon towns in Colorado, however, tend to be different from non-Mormon ones.

Any perceptive traveler can sense an architectural difference between Manassa and La Jara, Colorado. Part of the difference lies in the architectural style, with a higher percentage of central-hall plan types present in Manassa, and part lies in the retention of certain forms, such as arches and pediments on the older houses. Manassa and Sanford (another neighboring Mormon town) are distinctly different from nearby La Jara, although these towns were all founded at about the same time. The explanation—that the Mormons built their houses differently from those of the Gentiles—is a story repeated throughout the West. Fig. 43 attempts to represent the distribution of an architecture which is "Mormon" in character. It is partly based on subjective "feelings" received from firsthand observations, and partly upon fairly objective measurements such as house style, building materials, etc.

Mormon chapel architecture is also distinctive, even though several types of LDS chapels were observed. Their types vary through time rather than space. At first, there was no particular chapel style. Greco-Roman, Romanesque or rarely even Gothic forms can be seen. Most were simple, built of stone or brick. Of the newer, more standardized forms, three specific styles are found: 1) the chapel of Georgian design without steeple; 2) the chapel of Georgian design with steeple; and 3) the most recent, having a block-like steeple tower topped by a needle-like spire, resembling an inverted tuning fork.

Fig. 44 reveals that the traditional (Canaanville) ward chapel with a Georgian steeple or spire is the most common, but that the newer style with sharp steeple is becoming important. All of the chapels studied were of stone or brick. Stone is more common on the older chapels while red brick is most common on the Georgian chapels, and a red or tan pressed brick is seen most often on the newer examples. These chapels are distinctive. Though some of the older ones might be confused with churches of other denominations, the newer Georgian and needle spires are easily recognized as LDS.

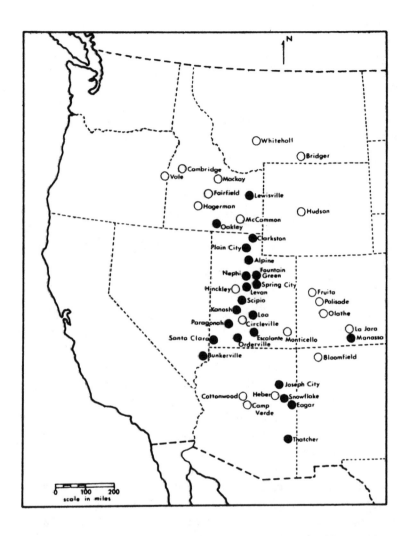

Figure 43.—Selected Towns in the Western United States: Mormon Architecture.

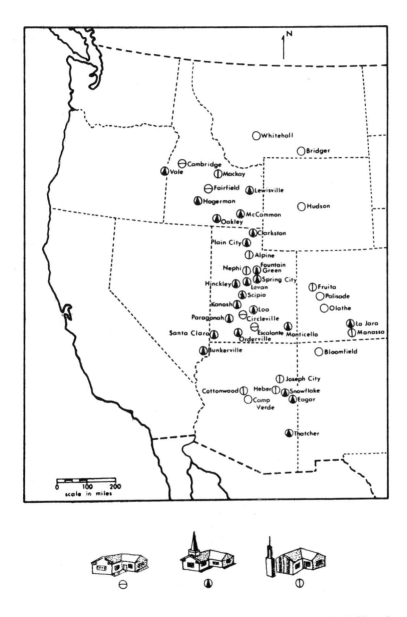

Figure 44.—Selected Towns in the Western United States: LDS Chapel
Styles.

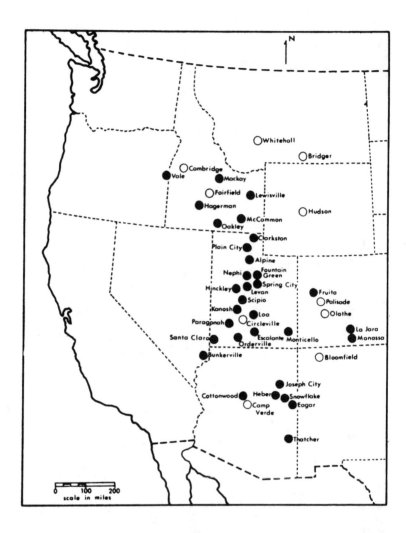

Figure 45.—Selected Towns in the Western United States: LDS Chapel Dominant.

LDS chapels have been placed in extremely dominant places, visually speaking, outside of Mormon towns in recent years. The 1950's and 1960's marked a period in which the LDS ward chapel began to appear along the main streets of non-Mormon towns. Vale, Oregon, and La Jara, Colorado, are examples of this. The Mormon church is gaining both in prestige and power in many western towns, and this distinctive Mormon landscape symbol has been diffused into parts of the West once considered Gentile strongholds, while remaining dominant in Mormon country itself (Fig. 45).

Several themes thus emerge from a spatial consideration of Mormon elements. First, certain elements are indeed "Mormon," for they appear only in Mormon country. The wide street, rural-village concept, barns and granaries in town, unpainted farm buildings and outbuildings, Mormon fences, and chapels are all important. Less so, but still significant, are elements such as the hay derrick, Lombardy poplar, irrigation ditches in town, etc. Second, it is possible to define, rather specifically, the area settled by Mormons by combining several of the traits, so that a visual delimitation, as well as a numerical population count, can be used to demarcate areas settled by the Mormons. That is how vividly different Mormon settlement was and is. This of course is dependent on the traits observed. Of particular note is that the Mormon landscape as developed at Canaanville is a classical pattern which depends on continuing Mormon occupation of a landscape primarily developed in the latter half of the nineteenth century. We shall soon see that both variables are extremely important.

A substantial portion of the western United States, then, bears the very real image of Mormonism. In fact, ten of the most significant factors can be used in delimiting Mormon settlement: 1) wide streets; 2) roadside irrigation ditches; 3) barns and granaries in town; 4) open landscape around the town; 5) architectural style (especially the central-hall house); 6) high percentage of brick homes; 7) the hay derrick; 8) Mormon fence; 9) unpainted farm buildings; and 10) the LDS

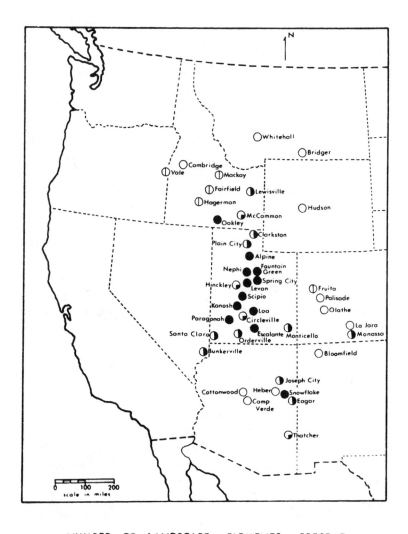

NUMBER OF LANDSCAPE ELEMENTS PRESENT

○ 0-1   ◐ 7-8
◫ 2-3   ● 9-10
◕ 4-6

Figure 46.—Selected Towns in the Western United States: Number of
Landscape Elements Present.

chapel. Simply stated, any town possessing more than five of these will be a Mormon town (Fig. 46).

THE LANDSCAPE THROUGH TIME

Dating of various features in a folk landscape has its inherent difficulties, the most severe being lack of documentation. According to the dates we could obtain, however—by discussions with townspeople, analyses of old photos and sketches, or appraisals of early descriptions—much of Mormon country has had its unique visual character for a long time. Some elements in the landscape have been present for a century or more. For example, virtually all towns were platted on the grid system, with wide streets. Ditches, too, were present in most towns since their earliest days. The public square dates from the town's inception. Even some of the old buildings on it were often built only a few years after the town's founding. Early chapels, Relief Society Halls,and tithing offices are often close to a century old.

The open fields surrounding many villages were likewise part of early Mormon planning and settlement. The location of barns and other outbuildings are also part of the early village plans. Many of the actual farm structures in towns date from before the turn of the century. Some were probably erected in the 1870's. The hay derrick probably made its first appearance about 1870. By the 1880's it was widespread and an important element in the agricultural landscape. A similar story could be ttold for the Lombardy poplar. Introduced in the 1860's, it spread throughout Mormon country by the 1880's. Mormon fencing was "developed" early, though it is merely the neglect or devolution of a common picket style. By 1900, fencing of most types seen today was present.

Dominant architectural forms, too, relate to the early days of many villages. Although primitive cabins and shelters were first built in most towns, these were soon replaced by substantial central-hall homes (and modifications of them). The Mormons built in similar styles from the 1850's until the turn of the century. This architectural character is related to the Mormons' early towns and farms in the "Old Northwest Territory" (especially Illinois and Ohio). After 1900 newer styles appeared, especially the more ornate Victorian. The newer ranch-style homes represent the most modern in village housing.

Religious architecture retains some old forms (especially the Greek Revival mode), but for the most part the newer chapels are radical abstractions of the simple Mormon architecture of older buildings. While the chapel harmonizes with the landscape because of its brick complexion and retention of Greek revival elements, it is nevertheless a bold new form punctuating the more ancient quality of farms and houses in the landscape. The unpainted aspect of Mormon farm buildings dates from the earliest days. The heavily weathered quality of wood in the landscape is the result of almost a century of weathering in the semi-arid climate.

Therefore, with the exception of a few newer buildings, street paving and replacement of irrigation ditches in some areas, much of the Mormon village landscape may be dated before 1900. Changes in agricultural systems, a growing impoverishment accelerated if not precipitated by the depression, and the rise of the automobile have all affected the landscape. But much of the architectural character of the town dates from an era dominated by self-sufficiency, cooperation, and use of animal power.

The early twentieth century marked a time in which new Mormon settlements began to lose much of their traditional visual characteristics. New towns settled after 1900, in fact, have a relatively poor development of the traditional features. The Mormon town of Heber, Arizona, is an example. The original Mormon settlers (ca. 1880) were forced to leave by a group of cattlemen. When they returned to build a new town in about 1915, they built one unrecognizable as Mormon. Heber, however, is not a farm village. It is primarily a sawmill town high in the mountains. But even newer agricultural areas settled after 1900 by the Mormons reveal a loss of many significant elements.

MAIN SOURCES OF ELEMENTS IN THE LANDSCAPE

Many of the elements in the landscape were brought into the West by the Mormons from their recently evacuated homes in the Old Northwest Territory. The early architectural styles (of chapels, homes and barns) are directly traceable to the American Midwest or East, and in some cases to Northwestern Europe. Many trees, shrubs and crops, too, were those that the Mormons had known in their old homes and had brought west with them.

Other elements were brought west as concepts, rather than as proven realities. The wide streets were apparently not built until the Mormons settled in Utah. Similarly, the plan for villages, with their separated fields and farm structures within town, first seem to have been institutionalized by the Mormons in Utah. These, however, are related to utopian concepts in planning that both Mormons and non-Mormons were familiar with in the Eastern and Midwestern United States. Nevertheless, the ideal plan found fertile ground in the isolated valleys of Utah, and became peculiarly "Mormon" in the West.

Certain elements in the landscape are more purely western, having been developed or adopted there after the arrival of the Saints. The hay derrick, for example, is a western implement. The use of adobe bricks was also a trait that the early Mormons were quick to utilize. These "Spanish bricks" as they were called, soon became an important building material in the early villages.

Thus, the Mormon landscape contains three main types of elements: those that had been present in the areas from which the Mormons had come; those that came west with them as concepts; and those that are unique to the semi-arid West either by invention or by the introduction of other

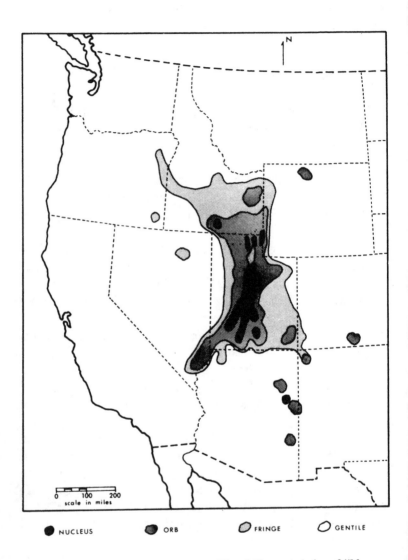

Figure 47.—The Western United States: Visual Characteristics of "Mormon Country."

peoples. The Mormon landscape is a combination of the familiar and the unfamiliar in the American scene.

THE LANDSCAPE: SPATIAL EXPRESSION

The distinctive landscape we see in the Intermontane West today was developed in the latter half of the nineteenth century (1850 to 1900), and is perpetuated by present-day Mormon occupancy. The landscape is unique, and can be broken down into several main parts, all related to the visual qualities present (Fig. 47).

The visual nucleus, or classical Mormon area, is well defined but composed of several areas, some connected, some isolated. The "Utah corridors" embodying the smaller villages set in the north-south trending valleys of the Rocky Mountains mark the epitome of this visual nucleus. The towns along Highways 89 and 91 are in reality valley-oases strung out like beads on a string. Scipio, Nephi, Levan, Paragonah, Fountain Green, Spring City, and Orderville form an important part of this visual region. This is the Mormon heartland. It once extended, unbroken, north through the Provo-Salt Lake City-Ogden region before urban dominance obliterated the rural landscape. Today in the Cache and Bear Valleys isolated remnants of that visual nucleus can be found. Farther north, into Idaho, are a few outlying areas that also are classically Mormon, but that are immediately surrounded by landscapes less dominated by the Saints. Oakley, Idaho, is well-developed and immediately recognizable as Mormon. South into Arizona, a few isolated examples of the visual nucleus are again to be found, places where the Mormon landscape looms into full view after being absent for several hundred miles. The Taylor, Snowflake, and Eagar (Arizona) areas exemplify this. Due to the division of the village into many small farms, this visual nucleus of Mormon country has a miniature scale reminiscent of New England. And, because of the presence of many elements relating to the use of animal power (old wagons, hay derricks, etc.), much of this central area is more late "eo-technic" or "horse-and-buggy" in character than the surrounding areas.

There is another, larger area which is also visually Mormon, but moderated. In this "visual orb" the important elements are either missing or more poorly developed, and the feeling is mitigated, although still "Mormon." The Monticello, Utah area, the Sanford-Manassa, Colorado area, and the Joseph City, Arizona area fit this description, as does Lewisville, Idaho.

Here one encounters fairly well-developed Mormon villages, but often the surrounding area contains dispersed settlement. In the villages themselves there is less of a "Mormon" feeling. There are fewer central-hall houses; brick may lose its dominance as a building material; the poplar may be but a minor element in the landscape.

Loosely surrounding this visual orb is a zone in which Mormon elements can be seen and recognized but are not combined to form any vivid impression of a truly unique landscape. The visual influence of Mormonism is minor in this fringe area.

In this visual fringe a Mormon hay derrick may be seen, but will often be near a freshly painted barn. Poplars may criss-cross the landscape and the LDS chapel may even be dominant, but churches of other denominations become important, too. Agricultural settlement becomes more dispersed. The self-sufficient village is not to be found here. Only here and there in the visual fringe is the feeling of Mormon country sensed. For the most part the perceptive traveler is in a disorienting zone representing a transition between the Mormon West and the non-Mormon West.

Salt Lake City and vicinity may still be the focal point of the Mormon religion, and its temple and wide streets have often been cited as Mormon, but its landscape has been so modernized as to resemble virtually all other large American cities. An occasional central-hall house is seen wedged between newer buildings, but clearly this is not a part of the visual nucleus today, in other words, Salt Lake City and vicinity turns out to be part of the visual fringe, ironically enough. Surrounding the visual fringe is the non-Mormon or Gentile West. Nothing that can be considered truly Mormon is found here, with the exception of an occasional isolated element. The three Mormon visual zones form, in fact, a large island, the boundary of which might be viewed as a zone of interchange, where Mormon traits push outward, as in the ward chapels, and where non-Mormon traits move into the Mormon area, such as the mechanical hay loader or the new, prefabricated metal silos and bins which are becoming more dominant yearly—pushing even into the heart of Mormon country. All zones of the Mormon landscape are in a state of flux. Modern technology presses inward, and old barns fall to the ground, crushed by the elements or by the bulldozer. The visual nucleus is becoming smaller and smaller.

The Mormon landscape, then, is an entity which is changing, but which exists in various degrees. In some areas the visual impact is unmistakable, while in other places it is merely hauntingly similar to certain things seen in the real center of Mormon country. By now we have given the concept "Mormon Country" a very real image, as epitomized in the visual nucleus. The symbol of that nucleus, Canaanville, becomes a symbol to the cultural geographer of the manifestation of the material culture of a group of people who had rather special ways of doing things. The Mormon landscape stands as a unique entity, a conscious transformation of the geography of America. The question is—how, and why, did they do it?

NOTES

1. F.Y. Fox, "The 'Mormon' Farm Village in Colorado," *The Improvement Era*, Vol. 46 (1943), p. 451.
2. Each architectural sample was taken by counting houses by style, color and building material; other details were often noted. Twenty-five houses were usually considered in detail in each town.

PART II

Creation of
the Mormon Landscape

CHAPTER 3

Why and How: Motives and Methods in the Creation of the Mormon Landscape

TOWARD EXPLAINING THE LANDSCAPE

Awareness of a landscape at once so uniform and unique is bound to excite the curiosity of the geographer and perhaps even that of the general traveler. Why and how did the landscape attain its unique appearance? Were religious motives involved? Were there other motives, also, such as cultural and economic ones?

Several scholars have dealt with the inception and diffusion of the Mormon grid pattern for villages.[1] That particular land pattern is of interest to us, but only as a framework for the other, even more characteristic elements in the Mormon landscape. We must here ask the question: Did the Mormon concept of planning reach beyond the planimetric division of land to include even the visual aspects of settlement, loosely termed "scenery" or "landscape?"

The implication made is that the Mormon church was deliberately trying to create a specific type of settlement pattern which could be sensed as belonging distinctively to the Latter-day Saints. As soon as Salt Lake City was firmly established, colonists began moving out into other valleys, effectively copying the pattern, and the appearance, of the prototype city. In 1936, the geographer Joseph E. Spencer noted that

> the mother community, Salt Lake City, did more than direct the spiritual and social aspects of growth, for in entirety it became the structural model upon which all other settlements were planned. The street plan, division of lots, allocations of church and school blocks, system of water canals, fort, architecture, home gardens and so on for the villages themselves, the allocation of fields, pasturelands, the planning of irrigation systems for the general farmlands; all was systematically copied as nearly as possible in every new settlement. It was a unique though almost deplorable example of an effort to stereotype a people. . . .[2]

This statement was perhaps the most significant contribution made by a geographer to the Mormon landscape topic. And yet even Spencer concerned himself with differences which resulted from diversity in the physical and cultural setting. He never substantiated that initial statement or discussed how those planning decisions were directed. Others, too, have more recently dealt with the negative theme of how variations detracted from the original planning, rather than with the uniformity which resulted.[3] Nor do several works which have dealt with the diffusion of Mormon influences consider this topic.[4] Indeed, the subject of the LDS landscape has been so neglected that virtually all scholars studying Mormon planning have failed to consider what Spencer hinted, namely, that the Mormon church may have had a conscious desire to create a distinctive visual system in the Mountain West.

RELIGIOUS MOTIVES AND THE CITY OF ZION

In the purely religious sphere, there definitely were motives which today can be discerned in the landscape, and which even continue to operate, albeit with diminished intensity. A careful investigation of church doctrine reveals that church leaders from the very inception of the Mormon religion to the present have made specific recommendations regarding the visual appearance of Mormon settlements. Some were specific, some were vague, but they all appear to have had some effect.

Most firmly rooted in Mormon religious doctrine is the general concept of the City of Zion, a concept which preceded the westward migration. Joseph Smith, in 1833, brought forth specific plans for the City of Zion, which was in turn based on a "city that lieth four square" repeatedly referred to in the Old and the New Testaments.[5] The strict north-south-east-west grid, while in general use in the Old Northwest Territory at the time of Smith's revelation, nevertheless was perpetuated in all Mormon settlements after 1833. Likewise, the nucleation of farm life in the village is also traceable to Smith: He "also evidently had in mind some kind of permanent agricultural belt around the city which would limit its ultimate growth."[6]

Smith's original plan for the City of Zion, however, went much further than general recommendations: It also provided for streets to be 132 feet wide, and for houses to be set back 25 feet from the street lines, thus, as Smith himself mentioned, ". . . leaving a small yard in front, to be planted in a grove, according to the taste of the builder; the rest of the lot for gardens." He further specified that ". . . all the houses are to be built of brick and stone."[7]

This communiqué, which transcended the division of space and indeed entered into the realm of visual or aesthetic planning, is perhaps the most important single document in the history of settlement of the West. The stipulation of the front yard for a grove, with garden space around the house, coupled with the order to build in brick and stone, goes far in explaining some important visual elements in the Mormon landscape: the solid masonry homes, the clumps and rows of trees, the intensively cared-for gardens. Smith's plan would account for the wide streets as well.

This basic plan of settlement, like the ideas of the Mormon

leader himself, did not die at the time of his martyrdom in
1844. Rather, Smith's devoted friend and follower Brigham
Young sought to carry out, as nearly as possible, Smith's
teachings:

> To his dying day, Brigham Young proudly maintained such
> deep loyalty to his leader. Joseph's ideas, his designs, the
> revelations of God to him, all these were studied daily and
> hourly by his supremely fearless and passionately devoted
> follower.[8]

Though certain changes were made in the basic plan in the
West, its specifications were important in creating the village
scene as we know it.

RELIGION AND REALITY: THE MOUNTAINS

But a striking and new dimension was to be added to the
City of Zion, that of its mountain backdrop. Even Joseph
Smith, before his death, is reputed to have asked Brigham
Young to prepare to take the Saints to the Rocky Mountains.[9]
The Mormons purposely moved into rugged areas secluded
from Gentile intrusions. President G. A. Smith, a leader who
was, in fact, as much or even more concerned with Mormon
settlement and its visual aspects than Brigham Young, told
the Saints in 1861:

> If the mountains were covered with beautiful timber, and
> plenty of grain could be raised without irrigation, there is
> no doubt but our enemies would overrun us, or at least make
> a great deal of trouble; but as it is, we inherit the chambers
> of the mountains: the rocks are our protection, and the
> oases of the desert our homes.[10]

The theme is biblical, a chosen but persecuted people
fleeing to the wilderness and building a kingdom. As Mulder
noted, it was the awareness of their settlement in Zion in the

mountains which helped to make the Mormons "a covenant folk like ancient Israel."[11] On another occasion G. A. Smith also said, "I thank the Lord for these deserts, rocks and mountains, for they may be a protection to us. And while our enemies are trying to exterminate us, Israel dwells safely in the tops of the mountains."[12]

Brigham Young likewise expressed the desire to locate in the isolated valleys surrounded by rugged mountains, which became, in effect, protectors of the Latter-day Saints. He told them in 1852:

> Ourselves and our friends can find a place for many years to come amid these wild mountain regions, where surrounds the health inspiring atmosphere, and the clear cool mountain rivulet winds its way from lofty and rugged eminences, presenting a scenery bold grand and beautiful, to some sequestered vale, where downtrodden liberty shall feel exalting aspirations, and contentment find repose.[13]

This might be perceived as a poetic adjustment to harsh reality. And yet, there can be no doubt that the Mormons deliberately sought to settle the valleys which were "isolated" by lofty peaks. They had, in fact, a specific plan for settlements, and this plan was based upon obtaining arable land and potable water in the valleys of the West. The mountains, as noted earlier, were very real sources of life. They were, in addition, constant reminders of the spiritual mission that the Mormons were fulfilling, the prophecy found in Micah (". . . the house of the Lord shall be established in the top of the mountains . . . ," Micah 4:1-5), Isaiah, and other Old Testament prophets.

PERPETUATION OF THE PLAN: GENERALITIES AT HIGH LEVELS

The Mormon villages in the West resulted from a number of directives issued by the church leaders. In addition to town platting, which was accomplished by members of the church appointed for that purpose and familiar with surveying, the church leaders had definite concepts of what Zion should look like. Brigham Young told his people:

> There is a great work for the Saints to do; progress and improve upon and make beautiful everything around you. Cultivate the earth and cultivate your minds. Build cities, adorn your habitations, make gardens, orchards and vineyards, and render the earth so pleasant that when you look upon your labors you may do so with pleasure, and that angels may delight to come and visit your beautiful locations.[14]

This is typical of the statements made by Young and other church leaders, such as G. A. Smith. Directives issued from the General Conferences in Great Salt Lake City were often aimed directly at the building and beautification of Zion, but were of a generalized nature: settlers were asked to "build up Zion," and to " build beautiful homes," but the specific details of construction were not stipulated. These directives were generalities which set the scene for an acceptance of more specific policies at the local ward level.

By far the most effective means of transmission of church policy regarding settlement was for an important leader, such as a member of the First Presidency, or even the President himself, to visit a community and offer suggestions or recommendations: Brigham Young's almost yearly visits throughout much of Zion were especially successful. During his visit to Wellsville, in Utah's Cache Valley, he told the Saints:

> Learn how to apply your labor. Build good houses, make fine farms, set out apple, pear and other fruit trees that will flourish here, also the mountain currant and raspberry bushes; plant strawberry beds and build up and adorn a beautiful city. . . .[15]

Brigham Young's role cannot be overestimated. Nor can the influence of other members of the church hierarchy, such as those in the First Presidency and in other powerful church positions. G. A. Smith was particularly important, and his speeches have been cited as a significant factor in the settlement of the Iron Mission in Utah.[16] Speeches such as the following, given at Parowan, Utah, on January 24, 1856, must have made a vivid impression on the people and, later, on the landscape:

> I feel anxious that you should begin to beautify Parowan, and make it like the garden of Eden. Set out at least 2,000 fruit trees, and more, if you can. . . . I would like to have you plant the public square to fruit trees, reserving a sufficient space for a public building in the center. I have seen your Tithing Office, and will say it is the best in the territory—the most substantial and well-furnished. You may fill it with grain without breaking it down. Cease to build temporary buildings, but put up those of a permanent kind.[17]

President John Taylor, Brigham Young's successor, also visited the Saints at their villages. He told the congregation at Malad, Idaho, on October 20, 1881, in tones very reminiscent of Brigham Young:

> Now, you who live in this little place, look to it that you are found in the line of your duty. You have a beautiful location, and I would like to see you make the most of it. I would like to see at least a hundred times more apple, pear and cherry trees planted out; and all of your streets lined with shade trees. And improve your dwelling houses. If you cannot find the style of a house to suit you, go off to other places until you do find one, and then come back and build a better one.[18]

This is a specific recommendation for the building and beautification of Zion.

The reference to "better dwelling houses" certainly meant permanent ones of masonry. G. A. Smith wrote a general statement in the *Deseret News* that "we have the finest kind of clay for making brick and adobies and plenty of lime so it will be our own fault if we don't build fine homes."[19] Amasa Lyman on one of his early visits to Parowan, Utah, (on September 14, 1856) showed the Saints gathered there how to build and ventilate brick homes, stating "I want you to build . . . as though you intended and expected to live here eternally. When you build your houses, build houses *to live in.*"[20]

There is ample evidence that the Saints followed these recommendations. But some did not. Since these recommendations were considered religious doctrine and not mere suggestions, those who did not obey were chastised. "Such neglect of duty," Brigham Young told the Saints at Salt Lake City in 1862, "is the very way to bring the power of the Devil upon us."[21] This warning was issued because Young noted a laxity in improvements, planting shade and fruit trees and building good homes. Needless to say, good Latter-day Saints would not want to suffer damnation, nor estrange themselves from their beloved leaders, whom they regard as men in direct communication with God.

THE LOCAL LEVEL: GENERALITIES INTO SPECIFICS

The historical records of many Sabbath meetings are rich in material relating to building and improving Zion. Often, visiting church members would give brief speeches and testimonies. For example, Elder M. McCune, returning to Nephi, Utah from a British mission, spoke to the Saints on April 20, 1854:

> I believe that I was lead [*sic*] by God to settle in Nephi. I allways [*sic*] felt that I loved the Saints of Nephi. May God bless you in your labors—I hope to see your meeting house [and] Social Hall—Better houses—and an improvement in all things—I hope to see your habitations embellished—flours [*sic*] cultivated—shade trees planted—a fit place for the angels to visit.[22]

This appears to be a "folk version" of a Brigham Young speech. It nevertheless captures the spirit of the building of Zion. The standard sought was for better public-religious buildings, planting of trees, gardens, etc. To attain that standard it was common to refer to other towns which had achieved a better appearance, or better development. Thus, at a Stake Conference meeting held at Loa, Utah, on May 30, 1897, Elder Lyman

> said he would present some thoughts upon this valley, he felt that all that could be done in putting out fruit and shade trees, spoke of Cainesvill [sic] and its planting trees . . . Wanted to see hard wood trees planting, and recommended this matter to the Bp [Bishop] —and leading men[t] to take this up, as the trees would help the good conditions along, he compared Loa to Panguish [sic] and some other places, he said the hardy fruit would grow here. . . .[23]

The bishop had a responsibility over his ward, the smallest effective unit in the church, and very often it was the bishop who recommended additions and changes at the grass roots level, even though main decisions originated at Salt Lake City. As Kate B. Carter noted, most of the settlers "willingly followed the path their leaders designated, yet the strength of the Mormon village was largely developed in community life, the center of which was . . . a combined church and school building."[24]

A bishop, using the meeting house as a community focal point, might instruct his people in temporal matters, as well as reaffirm church policy in Salt Lake City. Thus Bishop Henry Hunt of Cedar City, Utah, wrote to Apostle George A. Smith at Salt Lake City, saying "A little farm well cultivated near homes, I know, is your doctrine, and it is mine and ever was."[25] Smith had often expounded upon this principle.

Indeed, it was at the local meeting house that virtually all town planning occurred, and that numerous suggestions pertaining to more effective or more beautiful ways of doing things were made, both by the bishop and other members of

the priesthood. The meeting house became not only the out-
let for administrative decisions from Salt Lake City; it also
became the local center for the diffusion of ideas. The Metho-
dist minister and missionary Clayton Rice, living among the
Mormons at St. George, Utah, once complained, "Service Sunday [was] little more than a farmer's institute for half the
talk was about raising fruit, hogs and cattle."[26]

DITCHES AND FENCES: PROBLEMS ON SUNDAY

The problems of fencing and ditching are often mentioned
in Church historical records, for there was no effective sepa-
ration of religious and temporal matters. A meeting convened
at the Council House at Nephi, Utah, March 14, 1852 saw a
prayer by Br. David Webb and it was ". . . Motioned and
Caried [sic], that our fencing around the large field shall con-
sist of poles five to a pannel [sic] strait [sic] and of good size
sufficient to make a good substantial fence."[27] In the same
town, Bishop Bigler addressed the congregation on Sunday,
July 12, 1857. "Another thing I want to speak about is water-
ing," he said. He briefly discussed regulating water, and then
added, "Let no one meddle with the ditches after I have regu-
lated them, if you will do this it will save me pulling so many
brush heaps out."[28] One can find local bishops directing policy in Mormon towns at widely varying locales. Several members of the congregation in Snowflake, Arizona, undoubtedly
cringed on Sunday, October 14, 1888, when "Bp. John Hunt
. . . said he had been trying to keep the streets clean[;] spoke
very pointedly on this subject."[29] In Eagar, Arizona, we learn
that "Bp. Crosby spoke upon good fences, roads, etc." and,
he added, "We should build good buildings."[30] The bishop
united the village, and tried to establish church policy at the
local level. There was no "secular versus religious" conflict,
especially in the early days of settlement, since the society
was in fact a theocracy.

TRAVELING TREES: DIFFUSION AND THE CHURCH

Even the diffusion of plant and tree types from Salt Lake City to the smallest of towns was a deliberate result of church colonization. Simply stated, the first settlers brought plants with them to Salt Lake City: "George A. Smith brought peach stones and from them grew the first peaches which were given away liberally—one to a family and each stone planted a new tree."[31] Later, these trees spread when individuals—often appointed by the church—would be sent out to other towns. Thus it was that "James Starley was sent by Brigham Young to Fillmore in the spring of 1858 to establish a nursery. . . . It was very important that each small pioneer settlement be supplied with well trained nurserymen and horticulturists."[32]

Early records of many a small Mormon town note the beginnings of horticulture. At Mona, Utah, we find that "Edward Kay brought locust tree seeds from Salt Lake City and started the first shade trees from these seeds." His little grove, the historian tells us, supplied trees for other settlers as well.[33] As soon as the stock became well established in one town, settlers there could then spread trees to the next settlement by seeds or cuttings. Thus, at Levan, Utah, "Jacob Hofheins and William Morgan also planted fruit trees—apples, pears, peaches and plums. These trees came from Springville."[34] Trade in nursery stock soon developed into a barter system.

The Lombardy poplar, long considered a "Mormon Tree" was no doubt introduced and diffused in much the same way. An accepted account claims that the Lombardy poplar was brought to Salt Lake City in 1862 by the Englishman John Reading, and planted the next year in other parts of the city by William Wagstaff.[35] "Latter-day Saints probably first began to hear from one another about the Lombardy poplar at the general conferences of 1864 or 1865."[36] The tree was then probably brought to other villages by settlers; by the 1880's virtually all areas settled by the LDS were visually dominated by poplars.

The poplar was a beautiful tree, but motives for planting it must have been practical rather than purely aesthetic. It grows quickly and makes an effective wind break. Wallace Stegner has noted that poplars may have served as substitutes for hedgerows in the English landscape.[37] This is possible, since they effectively demarcate property lines. At the same time, the poplars are a vivid sign of settlement in the arid West. One can spot a settlement by their presence from several miles away.

Because the trees are so closely associated with Mormon settlement, and are so striking, it is tempting to ascribe some religious significance to them. They may be perceived as Gothic spires in a landscape virtually barren of conscious Gothic symbolism. Romanticizing the poplar to this degree is a relatively recent trend; in fact, the early Mormons left no record of such admiration. To them it was perhaps beautiful, but was only another tree with which to tame the desert and beautify Zion.

J. McClintock noted that "one of the first things the Mormons always did in establishing a new settlement was to plant fruit, shade trees and the like, so that in a very few years there was a condition of comfort only attained by a non-Mormon settlement after the lapse of a quarter of a century."[38] Indeed, this important task was often supplemented by other groups besides the "church" and its directives. It was in this spirit that many of the local "garden clubs" originated. All members were LDS and meetings were usually held in the LDS meeting house; there was no real attempt to remain autonomous. The main function of the St. George garden club, as stated in its records, was to "purchase, propogate [sic] and raise, choice fruits, nuts and vegetables, to make and own propogating [sic] gardens. . . ." The Nephi Farmers' and Gardeners' Club, organized in January 1870, had a similar purpose: "Its object shall be to incourage [sic] and improve stock raising, farming, gardening and importe [sic] seeds, plants and stock to that effect."[39] Many of these clubs are in existence today, but their main task appears to be "improvement" and "cleanup" rather than introduction of new varieties.

Even the Relief Society (a women's group and an integral part of the LDS church structure) helped, in days of old, to establish gardens and plant trees for the betterment of Zion. At Escalante, Utah, we find that "Around 1890 interest in silkworm culture was encouraged among Relief Society women of the LDS church in localities where mulberry trees thrived."[40] While the society participated in other facets of the building of Zion, its main task has been to manufacture items to raise money for the ward, and to make clothes for the dead.

REINFORCING DIFFUSION

The total result of this type of diffusion was to beautify Zion and create, again, a uniformity throughout the numerous settlements. Very much related and equally as effective was the way in which repetitive architectural expression was achieved in the earlier days of Mormon settlement. While the church had no specific architectural formulas—either for religious or secular building—it assured visual conformity by sending colonists from one place to another after they had spent only a short time in a particular place. Thus, an important part of the building up of Zion involved the church leaders selecting or "calling" individuals who had successfully settled one area to pick up stakes and move to another new Mormon community. The Mormon people were highly mobile even after their migration to the West. There are records of settlers moving three, four or even more times. Since carpenters, architects and others who made a significant impact on the landscape were included in these moves, it is not surprising that there is, architecturally as well as in other ways, a visual continuity throughout much of Mormon country.

As Chauncy Harris noted:

> The composition of the settlers for each village was also carefully planned. The building of a balanced group of settlers in each village . . . entailed selection with regard to previous training as farmers or artisans.[41]

Small wonder that a visual uniformity resulted! A look at
Gentile settlement in the West reveals no such selection, but
rather a relatively unrestricted flow of peoples toward economically desirable goals. Not to be underestimated is the fact
that all new Mormon settlers came through Salt Lake City.
The first scenes of Zion were here burned into the conscious-
ness of the new immigrant. Mecca had been reached.

Also related to religious doctrine, but very much tied to
cultural factors, was the way in which the church's proselyt-
ing campaign affected the landscape. Converts were actively
sought in the Old World, especially in England, Holland, and
the Scandinavian countries, while Brigham Young himself encouraged missionaries to seek artisans and others with building skills for conversion to the church.[42] These people who
came to Zion continued to build in styles and traditions with
which they were familiar. Even today one can note Old World
traits in the Mormon West, such as "Dutch" cross-bonded
brickwork, "Swiss" woven willow fences, and so on.

Accounts can be found of people who wanted to emulate
their Old World surroundings in the West. In Fremont, Utah,
the story is told of a widow, Mrs. Jenson:

> She was not satisfied with her home until she had built a
> rock wall around it, similar to those around homes in her
> native land Sweden. She built a rock wall, inclosing three-
> fourths of an acre around the home, with her own hands.[43]

The curious Old-World flavor of the Mormon landscape then,
was also related to the fact that the ethnic composition of
Mormon Country was indeed more "Old-World" than other
parts of the West.

SUBCONSCIOUS RELIGIOUS MOTIVATION

In the more "subconsciously" religious sense, the Mormons continued to build in styles reminiscent of Nauvoo and

their eastern homes because these places held religious connotations. Nauvoo had been associated with Joseph Smith and
the concept of the Holy City. Before their persecutions, their
toil had been expended to make Nauvoo perhaps the most
beautiful and certainly the largest city in Illinois at that time.
This could not be forgotten. Brigham Young, in preparing his
people for the grueling journey westward after they had been
driven from Nauvoo, told them in sarcastic terms:

> We will celebrate our perfect and absolute deliverance from
> the power of the devil—we only celebrate now our deliver-
> ance from the good brick houses we have left, from our
> farms, and lands, and from the graves of our fathers; we
> celebrate our perfect deliverance from these.[44]

Yet deliverance from the material side of life was far
from absolute. Those "good brick houses" were part of Zion,
as was the industry of the Saints that had gone up in flames.
Even if subconsciously, the Mormons would attempt to repro-
duce what they had had at Nauvoo, only this time in the shel-
ter of the mountains.

Bishop John Hunt at Snowflake, Arizona told his congregation on October 12, 1890, "I remember well the scenes at
Nauvoo. . . ." Elder Thomas Gottam at Bunkerville, Nevada
on September 1, 1901, brought the point home when he com-
plimented "the people of Bunkerville on their progress in temporal matters . . . he spok [sic] of the work in building up
Navoo [sic]. It was part of the religion of the L.D.S."[45] Thus,
the concept of Nauvoo remained ingrained in the Mormon
personality, and this positive factor expressed itself in con-
servative building in the West.

Significant, too, was the fact that the common people of
Deseret might want to emulate the architecture of their church
leaders; thus Brigham Young was "an encourager of an architecture which, though traditionally Colonial, was individual
and characteristic enough to be known as Brighamesque."[46]

Just how much copying of favorite homes occurred we will probably never know, but it is certain that

> "Gables, like that house in Palmyra"; "second story windows like the Lorenzo Snow home"; the "doorway like Elder Woodruff's home in Nauvoo"; "a porch like Brother Heber C. Kimball's", were all unquestionably influential in determining the appearances of homes in Utah.[47]

These influences spread to more than just Utah. The desire to emulate the pleasing elements of homes of other church leaders seen in places that were part of Zion spread southward into Arizona, Colorado and even northern Mexico; and northward into Idaho and Wyoming, as various craftsmen traveled through Deseret. Ralph Ramsey, a skilled Mormon who worked on Brigham Young's Beehive House in Salt Lake City, also left his carpentry mark on Mormon houses in Richfield, Utah, and Snowflake, Arizona. The fine brick homes at Snowflake, Arizona seem to have a uniformity about them. Most were built in a relatively short time (1888-1892) by Alan Frost and his sons, who had also worked in other Mormon towns.

TOOLS AND MEN

A repetition of visual forms occurred in the West, moreover, because the tools which built Nauvoo and other homes and cities of the early Saints were brought west. This is more purely cultural, but it is worth noting that, "as families firmed their attachment to a farm or city lot, the new house was undoubtedly conceived in the image of the old homestead in Nauvoo, Kirtland, Dresden, County Cork or Nottingham."[48] The architectural forms are reminiscent of the East, and even the Old World because "handbooks available to builders of the period were filled with Greek orders, Greek detail, Greek moldings, doorways, windows, etc. The molding planes which the journeyman joiner brought with him carried Greek profiles."[49] This helps to explain the similarity between East and West.

RELIGION: POSITIVE OR NEGATIVE?

Religion united the people and offered a framework upon which to build. That framework was the modified plan for the City of Zion in the spiritual setting of the mountain West. It is, therefore, surprising that religion in the purest and most positive sense was perhaps a relatively minor force in the creation of the landscape. More properly speaking, it was a religious framework within which already present cultural traits were developed that gave a unique character to the Mormon landscape. What the Mormon religion implicitly or explicitly prohibited, in addition to what it deliberately fostered, also helped to give Mormon country its unique appearance.

Many years ago the geographer Lucien Gallois discussed the Old-World, mature look of Mormon settlements. Chauncy D. Harris likewise noted this maturity, and attributed it to the fact that Mormon settlement "was the first settled of the major agricultural areas between the Middlewest and the Pacific Coast."[50] This is only a partial answer, however. Much more significant is the fact that the Mormon landscape is a result of an isolation, a deliberate retention of earlier cultural traits which were perpetuated long after they had run their course in the general Gentile culture at large. The religious motive to remain free from Gentile influences ("Babylon") pervaded Mormon ideology and resulted in a landscape which had passed from the American scene years before.

When Mormonism was founded, the Eastern and Midwestern portions of the United States were dominated by the Federal and Greek-Revival styles in architecture. At this time there was nothing especially distinctive about Mormon architecture, even at the "Holy City" of Nauvoo.[51] The Mormons brought the central-hall house to the West with them, and were especially enamored of the Greek Revival, with its heavy cornices and stress on simplicity of line. These were common forms in the Eastern landscape, as we have noted.

But very soon after their arrival in Utah it became apparent that Mormon architecture was stagnating. Markham, in his study of Utah architecture, mistakenly assumed that the Mormons "no doubt" after 1860 were influenced by the pattern books and magazines that affected the East and Gentile West.[52] There is no evidence of this. In fact, a survey of pioneer and early life styles in Utah revealed that very often the only books that Mormons possessed were religious, not secular. A typical response to the W.P.A. questionnaire was that the "Bible, Book of Mormon, Pearl of Great Price, and other church books" were the only ones available.[53] Architectural stimulation was, at this time, more internal than external.

It is true that the early Mormons were sociable (among themselves especially) and that they were fond of the theater and other "cultural" events. This should not be construed, however, to imply that Gentile ways were readily adopted. In fact, it was in the West, after severe persecutions drove them there, that Mormon leaders began to stress isolation from the Gentiles in both the religious and the secular sense. Brigham Young cautioned the Saints against associating with, or copying the ways of, the Gentiles.[54] On the more local level, at a meeting on May 30, 1898, the Saints at Escalante were told, "We came willingly to these mountains to be alone but today we cannot tell a Saint from an outsider, has [as] they are in [our] midst we partake of their habits but we should have prayers & make Zion." Several years earlier, on November 1, 1896, Elder Wright had told the Escalante Ward, "that the people of Escalante should be glad that they are isolated from the evils that the other settlement[s] have," and also "that we were gathered into the tops of the Mountains to serve the lord. . . ."[55] An ethnocentrism and in-group solidarity characterized (and characterizes today) the typical Mormon village.

It was at the Colorado Mormon town of Manassa that President Erastus Snow developed this theme of isolation as he spoke to the local Saints on August 24, 1879. He "occupied the time in instructing the saints in regard to their temperal [sic] duties, urging upon them to become self sustaining, and endover [sic] to build houses for themself [sic] and dose [thus?] become Independent of maney [sic] of the enfluences [sic] that now surrond [sic] them."[56] This is a specific recommendation to avoid Gentile trends in architecture, since folk building on the part of the Mormons was stressed. Even today one can note the radical difference in architectural style between Manassa and nearby La Jara, a Gentile town. La Jara saw a flowering of the Victorian and Gothic, while Manassa is easily recognized as Mormon by its older style of architecture.

RELIGIOUS ARCHITECTURE

A conservatism is noticeabe in religious architecture, as we might expect. Early ward chapels (and other ancillary religious structures) were of a simple Greek Revival style. They were, after the earliest pioneer days, almost invariably built of brick or stone. Though one might find quoins or a Greek pediment, the smaller Mormon religious buildings never were given the Gothic ornamental vocabulary of many contemporary Gentile churches. The work was usually simple. This prompted one author to write in 1947 that "the old stake tabernacles and ward houses built in obedience to the laws of proportion, form and design . . . are evidences again of a love of beauty, which always accompanies truth and the things of God."[57]

The Mormons have always stressed simple but effective houses of worship. An English artist, J. A. Hester, once noted that Mormon architecture "tended to do away with ornament and curves, depending on nice balances of flat areas for its effect."[58] Small, simple structures prevailed until the early 1900's, when church architects had a chance to unite many of the previously scattered religious functions into ward chapels. The newer ward chapels, which originated from the

church architect's office in Salt Lake City, maintained the
Mormon infatuation with the Greek Revival, an infatuation
that had long burned out elsewhere in the United States.

In 1914, Dr. Joseph Tanner, a Mormon, wrote in the offi-
cial LDS church magazine *The Improvement Era*: "We are in
religion as in our civilization generally coming to adopt a new
style of architecture, a style that is really ancient though ex-
pressing itself in newness of form." In what sounded like a
treatise on the virtues of Greek architecture as written almost
one hundred years before by Gentile architects, he added: "It
is the beauty of form. That beauty was first and highly expressed by the Greeks who learned the art of geometrical pro-
portions."[59] This epitomizes, too, a more general "Greek Revival" early in the twentieth century. But in contrast to other
religious groups, the Mormons became totally committed to it.

In that same issue of *The Improvement Era*, Lewis T. Cannon, architect, hinted that the church might develop a distinctive "Mormon" ward chapel architecture. He wrote: "The
Church of Jesus Christ of Latter-day Saints has not yet evolved
a distinctive type of architecture, but it may do so at some future time." He proceeded to state the various functions to be
fulfilled by the building—chapel, amusement hall, rooms for
the Mutual Improvement Association, classrooms, etc. He then
added, "It means also that the appearance of the building is considered, that it is made to minister to the aesthetic sense; in
other words, please the eye."[60] This statement set the scene for
his intimation that the church would deliberately become dominant in the visual affairs of the local community. His following
statement was: "The Church has gotten to the point in its history where it might with propriety exercise more of a supervision
or censorship, if you please, over the building of ward houses."

Just a few years after this statement, the *Deseret News* reported a "Distinctive Style of Church Architecture Developed." The article documented "the beginning of what may
be an L.D.S. chapel form of architecture has been brought to
the fore this year, for an effort is being made to establish in
all new ward chapels to be erected a type of building along

the line of the old colonial meeting house style."[61] The article perpetuated the myth that the basic style had been "brought to this country by the Pilgrim fathers . . ." and noted that the style had developed ". . . a purely classical type of simple, but purely symmetrical lines." The die was cast. Church architectects designed ward chapels of this type with amazing uniformity. Within a few years, the Mormon village landscape became dominated by this form.

A fine study of ward chapel architecture was done by K.W. Wilcox.[62] He noted the evolution, discussed the needs of the ward chapel; Cannon also offered astute observations on the use of space and the connotations of the resulting styles. The visual connotations of the Mormon ward chapel lend what is perceived to be a puritanical cast to the landscape. President Stephen L. Richards wrote in the *Deseret News* on October 25, 1953, "We don't build elaborately. . . . we don't build for show and ostentation, we build so that we may train ourselves in the truths that are everlasting and in the duties and obligations and opportunities that come to us in this glorious work."[63] The sober, substantial form of the multipurpose ward chapel is intended as a visual reminder of the well-ordered and constant demands that the church places on the life of the individual regarding worship, play, and cultural affairs. The chapel can be documented as a deliberate visual entity diffused by the church from its headquarters at Salt Lake City.

SYMBOLISM

The chapel and especially other church buildings are provided with rich but subtle Mormon symbolic vocabulary. (This, by the way, is a topic which has received virtually no attention from scholars, despite the importance of such symbolism in the landscape.) On the ward chapel spire is the circle or ring within a ring, a symbol of eternity. The more geometrical "L" and "V" symbols are also based on the square

and compass, which total 360° or the eternal circle. They had
their roots in Old Testament times. Together they signify
"spiritual light," and appear on the breastplate of the sacred
undergarment worn by every devout Mormon. Another ancient symbol is the Beehive, signifying industry. To the Mormons it symbolizes Deseret. It has now become secularized:
the Utah State Seal is a beehive, and this appears on many
highway signs. The religious connotation is still present beneath this modern-day veneer.

The all-seeing eye was originally a Semitic symbol depict-
ing the eye of God in the religious sense, or vigilance in the
more secular sense. It is used by other religions, but is preva-
lent among the Mormons. Stars are popular Mormon symbols
for the eternal order, or celestial kingdom. We noted their
appearance on tombstones. They also appear on the Salt
Lake City temple, as do all of the above symbols. The temple
itself is the doorway to heaven for the Mormons, and it appears as an obvious motif in Mormon country.

Mormon symbolism, like the religion itself, has a myste-
rious, almost "eastern" or Semitic quality about it, a quality
curiously reminiscent of the symbolism of the Masonic order.
In fact, a member of the Historic American Buildings Survey,
upon seeing the small endowment hall at Spring City, Utah,
with its "L" and "V" symbols, classified it as a "Masonic
lodge" having "Masonic emblem in gable end."[64]

An anti-Gothic trend runs through Mormon planning and
symbolism. This may be related to the deeply-rooted anti-
Catholic trends in the Mormon religion. Catholicism is rich in
symbolism of the Trinity, Christ's crucifixion, winged angels,
and other "graven images." These themes never appear visually
in Mormon country. The cross is non-existent; stained-glass
windows are rare on Mormon structures. Old Testament
themes are reflected in ancient symbols or in Mormon names
such as Nephi, Manti, and Moroni. Mormons visit the "temple" or "meeting house." They do not "go to church." The
New-Testament symbolism of 1500 years of Western Chris-
tianity is completely absent in the Mormon landscape.

THE CHURCH AND ITS ROLE TODAY

The ward chapels, it is true, are dominant in the landscape, but the interest that the Church once took in the general appearance of the village is no longer present. Even the definition of Zion has changed, from a specific place to an attitude. For the last few decades the Church has stressed building new chapels and improving older chapels and chapel grounds.[65] A typical result of the Church Beautification Program started in 1940 was that "the meeting house and Relief Society Hall were cleaned and painted, the Church lot was fenced, landscaped and beautified."[68] The remainder of the landscape has gone to seed, and the beautiful City of Zion as a concept is effectively dead, the local bishops apparently having no interest in perpetuating it.

The Church no longer stresses a mountain Zion as the only appropriate home for the Mormons. On the contrary, the Church is intimately associated with urban growth on the West Coast and has encouraged the establishment of wards elsewhere. And yet certain vestiges of the old visual pattern of Zion are occasionally retained. Mr. Leland Shelley, a contractor in Heber, Arizona, told me that all the streets in his new developments are about 66 feet wide, "almost twice as wide as the typical non-Mormon suburb." The inspiration for this was religious. Even though it is only half of the original 132-foot width for streets in the City of Zion, as Mr. Shelley noted, he felt that wide streets are a Church revelation which should be perpetuated. Generally, however, the Mormon concern for town planning did not survive much later than about 1900.

EXPLAINING THE CLUTTER AND SHABBINESS

We noted earlier that an important part of the Mormon village landscape is the ubiquitous clutter around the barnyard. If we follow the folk-culture observer who wrote, "It is possible to divide the world into two classes: the 'savers' and the 'throwers away,' " then the Mormons are clearly savers. While thrift of this type may be related to the "Protestant ethic" of rural American society, the Mormons must rate high. In fact, the cluttered appearance of the Mormon townscape has its roots, although they may be deeply subconscious, in the Mormon religion. The parable of the ten virgins (Matthew, 25:1-13) was, and is, a common theme at religious meetings. The Mormon theme: The wise save, and are prepared for the worst.

This is exemplified by the words of President Jesse N. Smith, speaking to the Snowflake, Arizona ward on October 2, 1890. He "said that all waste is wrong. The principle of economy underlies all the work of God. Let us save everything."[68] Widtsoe discussed the Mormon's frugality in relationship to their hard experiences, saying:

> Naturally, it became an ingrained habit to conserve everything of value. Waste was classified among the sins. . . . Using every effort in the battle with wind and weather, the care of the least and last of that produced, and the wise, frugal use of it, became a duty. . . . The old proverb, "Waste not, want not," was given a religious import.[69]

Even today the Church stresses keeping items such as old coal-burning stoves, in case of emergency. Many objects are kept because they "might be needed," and this goes a long way towards explaining why a hay derrick may stand for years—long after it is functionally obsolete.

The Church also requests that Mormons have at least two years' worth of food on hand—stored away in case of disaster. This helps to explain the solid cellars full of food, and also the substantial granaries. President Heber Kimball delivered an address to the Saints at the Tabernacle in Salt Lake City on March 9, 1856, in which he said:

> My feelings are, if God blesses and sustains me, to build a good storehouse for my grain this season; I am going to lay up everything I can raise. . . . Follow the example if you

think it a good one, and lay up stores of grain, against the
time of need, for you will see the time when there will not
be a kernel raised, and when thousands and millions will
come to this people for bread.[70]

Preparedness is a cherished virtue, even today.

This desire to save things has also been a problem since
the earliest days of settlement. In 1856, less than ten years
after the Saints arrived in the West, President G. A. Smith
told the congregation at Parowan, Utah, "to remove all Lumber, wood, hen houses, & c. to the rear of our houses and
keep our front yards and side walks neat and tidy." President
Pendleton also spoke on the same subject during the same
year, asking the Saints "to remove all wagons, . . . wood piles
& c. from the front of our houses and lots, to the back side
of our houses and lots. . . ."[71] In 1896, Patriarch E. J. Black-
burn chastised the Saints at Loa, Utah, when he "said the Ty-
phoid was caused by filtheyness [sic], of our surroundings;
and exorted [sic] the saints to clean up about our houses
and yards."[72] The frugal desire of the Saints, coupled with
their large lots convenient for storing "junk" of all sorts, has
long been a problem.

Another part of the landscape which has incurred the ire
of many citizens is the generally shabby look of the Mormon
farmyard, its unpainted crooked fences and aged unpainted
barns. Weedy streets and ditches are the rule.

Much of the look of the land, however, relates to the fact
that the villages are rather poor, and that the Church makes
very heavy demands on the individual in terms of time and
money. A percentage that might normally go to improvements is swallowed up by the tithe (10 percent). In addition,
the Mormon farmer often must raise his own money to send
his sons (or daughters) on missions, and he is often asked to
donate to other church causes. Likewise, time that might be
spent on repairs is usually devoted to the Church, which has
rigorous schedules for individuals even during the weekdays,
and effectively insures that no time will be available on the

Sabbath. The commandment, "Remember the Sabbath Day, Day, to keep it holy" (Exodus, 20:8) is strictly followed, and no devout Mormon works on this day. He attends priesthood meeting, sacrament meeting, and visits with other families. Small wonder, then, that the newer LDS chapel, funded about half by the community and half by the Church at Salt Lake City, raises its new spire above the relative poverty of the village.

Having little money to build with, and even less for repairs, the Mormon farmer uses what he has. Patchwork repairs are the rule. The barnyard, which was obviously of secondary importance compared to the home, is visible evidence of this. One study notes, "If the use of wood was shunned for the structure of the home, it was otherwise in the barn and corral. Here every limb and scrap from the sawmill were used as they generally are today."[73]

The hodge-podge variety of makeshift fencing in the Mormon village reveals at once the farmer's financial situation and his pragmatic response. Living fences were cheap and effective and had Old World roots. Rip-gut fences were perhaps the most primitive and certainly visually the most chaotic, but "wire was unobtainable and also expensive so fences were constructed from cedar branches placed rip-rap. However, they soon got the descriptive name of "Rip-Gut" fences."[72]

The "Mormon fence" is made of the cheapest materials available: scrap wood and slabs. It serves the purpose and does not seem to bother its creators, though visitors are often appalled by it. Mormon villagers soon learned that they were blessed (or cursed) with a lot of land to fence and not much money or time to spend on the task. They adjusted to this. Their fences are rustic and organic, but they do work.

The retention of almost all material things may be partially responsible for the ancient look of many villages. It is true that many elements in the Mormon landscape are truly Mormon, but the visual antiquity also stems from the fact that many things present in the landscape might have been torn

down years before in a non-Mormon town. An important part
of the character of the Mormon village is again related to Mormon frugality, pragmatism, and conservatism. The typical
Mormon town, as we saw at Canaanville, is something of an
outdoor museum.

ISOLATION

Adherence to the past is a result of deeply rooted Church
policy. Since self-sufficiency was from the outset a desired religious goal, the Mormons have in part been "isolated" from
the main trends in agriculture in the Western United States,
especially in the visual nucleus of their region. They may be
ready acceptors of new traits in some areas, but a deep rural
conservatism still persists in the heartland. Indeed, self-sufficiency and pragmatism have often partially dictated what
types of land use and construction techniques would be util-
ized, both in farm and field.

The Mormon desire for self-sufficiency in agricultural pro-
duction may still be seen in the landscape. Missing from the
landscape is the heritage of almost half a century of warring
between sheepherders and cattlemen. Sheep and cattle are
seen together because there was little or no competition between villagers for grazing land. Nor were livestock as segre-
gated as they were in the non-Mormon West, for herds were
often driven to a large enclosed pasture and grazed together.
Indeed, Brigham Young expressed no concern about the practice that sheep and other stock were being herded on his
farm.[75] Throughout much of Mormon country there is no
stigma attached to this practice, while in most of the West it
is regarded as inherently bad land use.

The Mormons do have different ways of doing certain
things, and their seeming apathy toward customs considered
by others to be proper or aesthetically pleasing has sometimes
put them at odds with the "modern" world around them.

A BATTLE IN ZION

A tremendous battle has resulted, in Utah especially, for many people find the Mormon townscape to be appalling, while others think it is colorful, rustic and "folky."

A report to the Utah State Historical Society in 1960 wrote of Escalante, Utah: "The town shows little if any civic pride. . . . The town has dirt and gravel streets, . . . Weeds seem to have the streets to themselves between the trails that are used for sidewalks and roadways. It is a common sight to see stray animals grazing along the city streets."[76] This complaint is common enough. And to compound matters, many inhabitants of the town don't find any reason to get upset about the rural, shabby quality. One story relates to a visitor who drove into Escalante and was disturbed to see fellows whittling and talking in town:

> Considering the broken fences and general rundown look of many houses, a visitor was once disturbed by the situation. After contemplating a group of whittlers, he asked irritably, "Is this all you fellows have to do?"
>
> No one answered for a minute. Then Hyme Bailey looked up and drawled, "We don't even have to do this, mister, if we don't want to."[77]

Dr. Arvin Stark, horticulturalist at Utah State University, finds the run-down condition of Mormon towns deplorable. He has actively campaigned for improvement and cleanup, and has even published a "Landscape Improvement Kit." Dr. Stark once said of his fellow Mormons, "We are so busy trying to get to heaven that we let our places look like hell." He advocates community cleanup and ripping down many old barns.

Actually, the movement is an old one, and as early as 1914 Alice M. Horne put the question to the Mormon villagers this way:

> What would you think of an ordinance to compel residents
> or land holders to keep out weeds? . . . What would weekly
> moving of garbage and manure bring about? . . . what gives
> more joy than a clean and beautiful home, a clean and beau-
> tiful yard, a clean and beautiful city? [78]

In some places, the beautification programs, some of which are said to have had their inception in the "Keep America Beautiful" campaigns sponsored by Lady Bird Johnson, have drastically transformed villages. Streets are mowed. Large holes fill the landscape where barns once stood. Fences are of the "modern" variety. In a very real way, much of the character of the Mormon landscape has thus been removed.

Realizing that there is a great deal of flavor to such a landscape, a more recent group has actively begun to campaign for preservation of the landscape heritage. In an article in *The Herald Journal* (Logan, Utah), Austin Fife, the Utah folklorist, deplored the fact that:

> One town in Utah is engaged in a vicious campaign to tear
> down all its barns. For the benefit of the non-Utahn, the
> small, weathered barns of the state are one of its architec-
> tural ornaments. Why, if you tear down those barns, you're
> gutting the town. [79]

In 1969, with the help of the Utah Heritage Foundation, Fife began a movement to help preserve the quaint heritage of the Mormon village. He stated his position to the *Herald Journal*: "Material culture—things like old stone houses, barns and fences of Utah— . . . These are the things that last, and the things that tell us what a civilization is."

The conflict partly has its roots in the subconscious awareness that Mormon towns "shouldn't look like this," since Mormon folk mythology stresses that the Mormons are cleaner than others. In some cases, there is an ignorance that Mormonism is a factor in the look of the town. Whatever the case,

"Utah town" rather than "Mormon town" safely connotes cultural rather than religious motivation. In only a very few cases does preservation of an entire town relate to its Mormon heritage.[80] This is because not everyone knows, or cares to admit, what a Mormon town really looks like. It is with this in mind that we enter the third facet of our discussion: perception of the Mormon landscape by travelers, artists, and even inhabitants of Zion.

NOTES

1. Nelson, *The Mormon Village*; and Sellers, "Early Mormon Community Planning."
2. Spencer, "The Middle Virgin River Valley," p. 90.
3. See J. A. Gedes, "Modifications of the Early Utah Farm Village," *Yearbook of The Association of Pacific Coast Geographers,* Vol. 8 (1942), pp. 15-22; and J. H. Baum, "Geographical Characteristics of Early Mormon Settlement" (unpublished M. A. Thesis, Brigham Young University, 1967); this was also a theme developed by Robert Layton in a paper entitled "The Mormon Village," presented at Salt Lake City, Utah, as part of the Rocky Mountain and Great Plains section of the Association of American Geographers, October 10, 1969.
4. J. E. Ricks, "Forms and Methods of Early Mormon Settlement in Utah and the Surrounding Region," *Utah State University Monograph Series,* Vol. 11, No. 5, (1964); also Charles S. Peterson, "Settlement of the Little Colorado, 1873-1900: A Study of the Processes and Institutions of Mormon Expansion," (Unpublished Ph.D. dissertation, University of Utah, 1967).
5. J. W. Reps, *The Making of Urban America: A History of City Planning in the United States* (Princeton: Princeton University Press, 1965), p. 472; and Sellers, "Early Mormon Community Planning," p. 25. Some examples of Biblical cities are found in Numbers 35:1-5 and Leviticus 25.
6. Reps, *The Making of Urban America,* p. 468.
7. K. B. Carter, "The Mormon Village," *Treasures of Pioneer History,* Vol. 14 (1955), p. 135.
8. S. Y. Gates, "Reminiscences of Brigham Young," *Improvement Era,* Vol. 11 (1908), p. 618.

9. D.W. Evans, J.W. Taylor, and J.Q. Cannon, "Discourse by Elder Orson Pratt, Delivered in the New Tabernacle, Salt Lake City, Sunday Afternoon, June 15, 1873," *Journal of Discourses by President Brigham Young, His Counsellors, The Twelve Apostles, and Others,* Vol. 16 (1874), pp. 79-80.

10. G.D. Watt and J.W. Long, "Prosperity of Zion &c., Discourses Delivered by Elder George A. Smith, in the Tabernacle, Great Salt Lake City, March 10, 1861," *Journal of Discourses Delivered by President Brigham Young, His Two Counsellors, The Twelve Apostles, and Others,* Vol. 9 (1862), p. 71

11. W. Mulder, "The Mormons in American History," *Bulletin of the University of Utah,* Vol. 48 (1957), p. 14.

12. Historical Records of Parowan, Utah, 1856-1859, (August 23, 1857) p. 25, Salt Lake City, Church Historian's Office.

13. P. Nibley, *Brigham Young, The Man and His Work* (Salt Lake City: Deseret News Press, 1937), p. 181.

14. Nibley, p. 181.

15. Nibley, p. 360.

16. R.H. Gleave, "The Effect of the Speaking of George A. Smith on the People of the Iron Mission of Southern Utah," (unpublished Master's Thesis, Brigham Young University, 1957).

17. Historical Records of Parowan, Utah, 1856-59, p. 3. Salt Lake City, Church Historian's Office.

18. G.F. Gibbs and J. Irvine, "Discourse by President John Taylor, Delivered at Malad, Oneida County, Idaho, Wednesday Morning, October 20th, 1881," *Journal of Discourses by John Taylor, President of the Church of Jesus Christ Latter-day Saints, His Counsellors, The Twelve Apostles and Others,* Vol. 26 (1886), p. 111.

19. *Deseret News,* April 29, 1851, p. 38.

20. Historical Records of the Parowan Stake, 1856-59, p. 19. Salt Lake City, Church Historian's Office. The underscorings are the recorder's.

21. Nibley, *Brigham Young,* p. 378.

22. Historical Records of Nephi, Utah, 1851-1862. Salt Lake City, Church Historian's Office.

23. Historical Records of Loa, Utah, 1894-98. Salt Lake City, Church Historian's Office.

24. Carter, "The Mormon Village," p. 138.

25. N.G. Woolsey, *The Escalante Story: A History of the Town of Escalante, and Description of the Surrounding Territory, Garfield County, Utah, 1875-1964* (Springville, Utah: Art City Publishing Company, 1964), p. 106.

26. C. Rice, "Thoughts, Experiences and Stories of Others in Utah." Diary no. 1, from July 10, 1908 to November 29, 1909, p. 8. Unpublished manuscript, University of Oregon Special Collection.

27. Historical Record of Nephi (Utah) Ward, 1851-1862. Salt Lake City, Church Historian's Office.

28. Historical Record of Nephi (Utah) Ward, 1855-1862, p. 61. Salt Lake City, Church Historian's Office.

29. Historical Record of Snowflake, Arizona, Book C, 1888-1891, p. 27. Salt Lake City, Church Historian's Office.

30. Historical Record of Eagar (Arizona) Ward, 1888-1894, Oct. 5, 1890, p. 53. Salt Lake City, Church Historian's Office.

31. A. M. Horne, *Devotees and Their Shrines: A Handbook of Utah Art* (Salt Lake City: Deseret News, 1914), p. 157.

32. S. H. Day and S. C. Ekins, *Milestones of Millard: 100 Years of History of Millard County* (Springville, Utah: Art City Publishing Company, 1951), p. 196.

33. A. P. McCune, *History of Juab County: A History Prepared for the Centennial of the Coming of the Pioneers to Utah, 1847-1947* (Springville, Utah: Art City Publishing Company, 1947), p. 140.

34. McCune, p. 154.

35. W. C. Patrick, "Poplar Trees are Happiest," *The Salt Lake Tribune*, November 12, 1950, sec. M, p. 1m.

36. S. Anderson, "Utah has snubbed a Friend," *The Salt Lake Tribune*, September 6, 1953, p. 9m.

37. Stegner, *Mormon Country*, p. 21.

38. J. H. McClintock, *Mormon Settlement in Arizona: A Record of Peaceful Conquest of the Desert.* (Phoenix: Manufacturing Stationers Inc., 1921), p. 128.

39. "Agreement of the St. George Gardners' Club," February 16, 1873, part 2. Salt Lake City, Utah Historical Society; Nephi Farmers' and Gardners' Club, 1883-1894, p. 1. Salt Lake City, Church Historian's Office.

40. Woolsey, *The Escalante Story*, p. 114; Relief Society Women's Auxiliary of the Church of Jesus Christ of Latter-day Saints, *A Centenary of Relief Society: 1842-1942* (Salt Lake City: General Board of Relief Society, 1942), p. 71.

41. C. D. Harris, *Salt Lake City: A Regional Capital* (Chicago: University of Chicago Libraries, 1940), p. 118.

42. J. A. Olson, "Proselytism, Immigration and Settlement of Foreign Converts to the Mormon Culture in Zion," *Journal of the West*,

Vol. 6 (1967), pp. 189-204; M. B. DeGraw, "A Study of Representative Examples of Art Works Fostered by the Mormon Church with An Analysis of the Aesthetic Values of These Works," (unpublished M. S. Thesis, Brigham Young University, 1959), p. 2.

43. A. Snow, *Rainbow Views: A History of Wayne County* (Springville, Utah: Art City Publishing Company, 1953), p. 187.

44. Nibley, *Brigham Young,* p. 187.

45. Historical Records of Snowflake (Arizona), Book C, 1888-1891, p. 135. Salt Lake City, Church Historian's Office; Historical Records of Bunkerville (Nevada), January 11, 1879 to September 22, 1901, p. 169. Salt Lake City, Church Historian's Office.

46. S. K. Yonemori, "Mahonri MacKintosh Young, Printmaker" (unpublished M. A. Thesis, Brigham Young University, 1963), p. 7.

47. F. L. Markham, "Early Architecture, 1847-1870," unpublished manuscript, Utah Historical Society, 1963, p. 3.

48. Markham, "Early Architecture, 1847-1870," p. 2.

49. Markham, p. 21.

50. See L. Gallois, "L'Utah," *Annales de Geographie,* Vol. 22 (1913), p. 118; Harris, *Salt Lake City,* p. 40.

51. R. M. Lillibridge, "Architectural Currents on the Mississippi River Frontier: Nauvoo, Illinois," *Journal of the Society of Architectural Historians,* Vol. 19 (1960), pp. 109-114.

52. Markham, "Early Architecture, 1847-1870," p. 3.

53. D. K. Owens, "Pioneer Personal Interview with Henry Excell," Nov. 16, 1938, p. 6, Utah State Historical Society, WPA Questionnaire Files.

54. Nibley, *Brigham Young,* p. 149.

55. Historical Records, Escalante Ward, 1892-1900, pp. 302 and 199. Salt Lake City, Church Historian's Office.

56. Historical Records, Manassa Ward, Book A, 1877-1879, p. 29. Salt Lake City, Church Historian's Office.

57. J. A. Widtsoe, *How the Desert Was Tamed* (Salt Lake City: Deseret Book Company, 1947), p. 59.

58. D. L. Morgan, *Utah: A Guide to the State* (New York: Hastings House, Publishers, 1941), p. 186.

59. J. Tanner, "Architecture in Religion," *The Improvement Era,* Vol. 17 (1914), p. 790.

60. L. T. Cannon, "Architecture of Church Buildings," *The Improvement Era,* Vol. 17 (1914), pp. 793, 796.

61. "Distinctive Style of Church Architecture Developed," *Deseret News,* Dec. 17, 1921, p. 29.

62. K.W. Wilcox, "An Architectural Design Concept for the Church of Jesus Christ of Latter-day Saints." (unpublished M.A. Thesis, University of Oregon, 1953).

63. S.L. Richards, "Chapels and Temples Held Monuments to Progress of Man," *Deseret News,* October 25, 1953, pp. 1-2.

64. P. Goeldner, *Utah Catalog, Historic American Buildings Survey* (Salt Lake City: Utah Heritage Foundation, 1969), p. 66.

65. M.O. Ashton, "Stop! Look! Listen!", *The Improvement Era,* Vol. 46 (1943), pp. 526-527.

66. A. Snow, *Rainbow Views,* p. 220.

67. F. Lichten, *Folk Art of Rural Pennsylvania* (New York: Charles Scribner's Sons, 1946), p. v.

68. Historical Record, Book C, Snowflake Ward, 1888-1891, p. 132. Salt Lake City, Church Historian's Office.

69. Widtsoe, *How the Desert Was Tamed,* p. 50.

70. G.D. Watt, "The Devil to be Cast Out of the Earth—The Emigration Fund—Exhortation to Bishops—Laying Up Stores Against a Time of Need. A Discourse by President Heber C. Kimball, Delivered in the Tabernacle, Great Salt Lake City, March 9, 1856," *Journal of Discourses by Brigham Young, President of the Church of Jesus Christ Of Latter-day Saints, His Two Counsellors, The Twelve Apostles, and Others,* Vol. 3 (1856), p. 253.

71. Historical Records, Parowan Stake, 1856-1859, pp. 11, 25. Salt Lake City, Church Historian's Office.

72. Historical Records, Wayne Stake, 1895-1901, p. 117. Salt Lake City, Church Historian's Office.

73. D. Winburn, "The Early Homes of Utah: A Study of Techniques and Materials" (unpublished B.A. Thesis, University of Utah, 1952), p. 18.

74. A.J. Levine, *Snowflake: A Pictorial Review, 1878-1964* (Snowflake, Arizona: By the author, 1965), p. 41.

75. Personal letter from Brigham Young to President Ezra Benson and Bishop Peter Maughan, Logan, Utah, August 7, 1865. Letter File, Utah State Historical Society.

76. D. Spencer, "A History of Escalante," unpublished manuscript, Utah State Historical Society, p. 20. See also Utah State Institute of Fine Arts, *Report on the Fine Arts in Utah, 1968* (Salt Lake City: University of Utah, 1968), pp. 47-50.

77. Woolsey, *The Escalante Story*, p. 389.

78. Horne, *Devotees and Their Shrines*, p. 156.

79. R. Nelson, "Makes Appeal for Old Things," *The Herald Journal* (Logan, Utah), November 13, 1969, p. 2.

80. R. C. Mitchell, "Obscure Spring City Utah Williamsburg?" *Deseret News*, March 11, 1968, pp. 5-7.

PART III

Perception and
Interpretation of the Landscape

CHAPTER 4

The Mormon Landscape in Art and Literature

For more than a century travelers, historians, artists and observers of the West have made comments on the Mormons and their settlements—some flattering, some critical. Since the Mormons were such a dynamic and unique group, we would naturally expect this. Yet, underlying most of the descriptions of Mormon settlement is the awareness that there was, and is, something distinctive, something different about it.

What elements in the scenery of the Intermontane West have observers recorded as "Mormon"? What, to them, comprised the Mormon landscape? Critics and observers were plentiful from the very beginnings of Mormon settlement, and soon after the Saints' arrival in Utah, writers and artists began recording the LDS scene on paper and canvas. They tell of a settlement type different from that in other parts of the West, stressing repeatedly several important elements which can be considered Mormon.

THE WRITTEN WORD

An early and perhaps typical description of Salt Lake City, the first Mormon settlement, was offered by Dr. James Schiel,

who visited the area in 1853-54 on the Gunnison-Beckwith
expedition into the West. He gives a vivid description of the
young town:

> The large City of Salt Lake lies . . . at the foot of the Wa-
> satch Mountains . . . it has a friendly appearance. Although
> the streets are straight and broad and almost every house
> has a plot of land with a fence around it, the city has a pov-
> erty-stricken and temporary appearance. The streets have
> sidewalks, that is, they have walks separated from the road
> by ditches, but they are just as impassable during bad
> weather as the roads themselves. . . .
>
> The above mentioned ditches also serve the purpose of
> conveying water from City Creek to all parts of the city;
> a very convenient arrangement for the inhabitants. Most of
> the houses are built of adobe. They have only one story,
> and the roof is made of shingles. . . . In the center of town
> there are several two-story houses, . . . the tithe-house
> (Zehnthaus), and the state house.[1]

This description cites the straight, wide streets, irrigation
ditches, small adobe houses with large lots around them, and
the central area of town, with larger homes, tithing house and
public building. Even in its infancy Salt Lake City was a good
example of Mormon planning, with a central area for public
and religious buildings.

Sketches of Salt Lake City in its early days show a sprawling, open landscape with small simple homes of frame and
adobe, orchards and gardens planted around those homes,
very wide, straight streets with ditches along their sides; a pro-
fusion of rail and post fences; trees of both fruit and shade
varieties, as well as the columnar Lombardy poplar rising
against a backdrop of the rugged Wasatch Mountains. The il-
lustrations in Stansbury's *Expedition to the Valley of the
Great Salt Lake of Utah* are typical in this respect. During
the 1850's Salt Lake City, like the other Mormon towns which
were then springing up in the Intermontane West, was an in-
fant but still had features recognizable as related to Joseph

Smith's careful planning of the City of Zion with additions and modifications by Brigham Young.

Some years later, in 1861, Mark Twain made his way through Salt Lake City, and offered his caustic comments on the Mormons, their beliefs and doctrines. His remarks on their landscape, however, reflect an underlying admiration of their works. Twain described:

> block after block of trim dwellings, built of "frame" and sunburned brick—a great thriving orchard behind every one of them, apparently—branches from the street stream winding and sparkling among the garden beds and fruit trees—and a general air of neatness, repair, thrift and comfort, around and over the whole.[2]

Twain was aware of the gardens and fruit trees, irrigation streams along streets, and trim dwellings. A year after Twain had visited Salt Lake City, the Englishman Richard Burton published his account of the Mormons, based on his observations of 1860. He mentions that "the farm houses with their stacks and stock, strongly suggested the old country," and that he "could not but be struck by the modified English appearance of the colony."[3] He also mentioned "the dark clumps and lines of bitter cottonwood, locust, or acacia, poplars and fruit trees, apples, peaches and vines, and noted that "the houses are almost all of one pattern, a barn shape, with wings and lean-tos, generally facing, sometimes turned endways to the street . . ."[4] Architecture is, therefore, cited as distinctive. As R. West noted, in the 1850's and 1860's "all houses now were constructed with English style roofs and gables"[5] lending a curious air to the desert city.

At the end of the 1860's the *Deseret News* reports that a visitor, A. K. McClure, described Salt Lake Valley in this manner:

> I have now spent a week with the Latter-day Saints, admired their green shades, beautiful artificial streams, pleasant homes and the innumerable evidences of industry and prosperity which appear on every hand.[6]

Again, mention is made of the trees, irrigation streams, and homes, as well as the almost intangible element of "industry" perceived in the landscape.

Joel Ricks, in his study of the "Forms and Methods of Early Mormon Settlement in Utah and the Surrounding Region, 1847 to 1877," described Salt Lake City in the following way:

> In the "60's" some of the newer buildings were built of stone, red bricks or lumber. Trees and shrubbery were planted in the front grounds to beautify the landscape and provide shade; in the rear, beyond the houses, gardens were cultivated. The waters of City Creek were brought by means of irrigation ditches to provide drinking water, to mature the crops, and to nourish the trees and shrubbery. Lombardy poplars were planted along the sidewalk for shade and beauty.[7]

As Mormon settlement spread, much the same scene could be recorded at many of their towns in the Intermontane West. Florence A. Bailey, in describing a small unnamed Mormon village along the Wasatch front north of Salt Lake City, tells us:

> It was a typical Mormon village, one of a line of closely connected settlements running along the valley between the Wasatch and the great lake. The settlements,—with their elaborate system of irrigation,— . . . afford examples of Brigham Young's shrewd policy of centralization.
> . . . Many of the streets were lined with locust-trees.
> . . . Under the trees ran mountain brooks, falling in white cascades down the hilly streets. Picturesque low stone houses were set back in bushy yards, each house with its orchard beside it,—delightful old overgrown orchards, in which the children played and calves grazed in the dappling sunlight.[8]

These are much the same things recorded earlier for Salt Lake City, and there is that additional stress on substantial architecture and lush, verdant appearance. This description of Snowflake, Arizona, also from 1894, is typical:

> As the traveler approaches Snowflake on the Woodruff road from the north he is apt to be favorably impressed with the appearance of the settlement. Clustered around the stake house (the spire of which, though not very lofty, points gracefully toward heaven), the stranger at once notices a number of fine brick dwellings and business houses standing in the midst of young, thrifty orchards, while the town itself is surrounded by well cultivated fields, properly fenced and systematically laid out by the respective owners for irrigation purposes.[9]

The stake house becomes the religious center of a neat, rural village. Less than ten years later another traveler also described the same village thus:

> The wide and neat streets with shade trees and running streams of pure water on either side, the large and substantial brick dwelling houses with vast green lawns and orchards informs the visitor, without further inquiry, that the inhabitants of the place are a progressive, energetic, prosperous liberty-loving and God-fearing people.[10]

These descriptions of Snowflake stress substantial architecture, irrigation ditches at the sides of wide streets, rural quality of town life as expressed in orchards and gardens, and again that "productive," "progressive" air so often referred to in earlier descriptions, but which becomes increasingly rare after the turn of the century. Later descriptions continue to stress the same landscape elements, but the air becomes sleepier, more relaxed. The traveler Clifton Johnson gives us this description of a Utah Mormon village in his book on western travels.

> It was an old-fashioned little place—one of the early settlements near the shores of the Great Salt Lake. Close behind rose a steep, lofty mountain ridge. Tall Lombardy poplars

lined the streets and stood in stately rows along the borders of the fields, while the houses nestled amid apple, cherry, peach, and other fruit trees. The dwellings were apt to be small, but their vernal setting of trees and vines made them quite idyllic. Irrigation ditches networked the whole region, and the life-giving water flowed in swift streams on one side or the other of every street. In the open country roundabout were broad acres of wheat and alfalfa, and luscious pastures.[11]

Mountain backdrops, tall poplars, shade trees, irrigation ditches and greenery are all an important part of this verbal picture.

A more critical observer, the geographer Joseph Earle Spencer, likewise noted elements in a scene which tend to characterize many Mormon villages in Utah:

[In each village] the streets were wide and almost invariably lined on both sides with irrigation ditches which brought domestic and irrigation water to every lot. . . . Shade trees of many sorts lined the streets, supported by the water of the ditch lines. In planning village sites, each home-plot was purposely made large, ranging from half an acre to an acre, in order to accommodate a kitchen garden and orchard, as well as barns, storehouses, and pens for livestock. Nearby fields were usually small in size, with larger or additional fields at a distance.[12]

While this description is not a "colorful" one, it too brings the feeling of order, verdure, irrigation and surrounding fields as part of Mormon village "character."

The famous Western historian Wallace Stegner was so impressed by the Mormons' effect on the land that he wrote *Mormon Country*. He was very much aware of the visual impact of the Mormon village when he noted:

Wherever you go in the Mormon country . . . you see the characteristic marks of Mormon settlement: the typical intensively-cultivated fields . . . the orchards . . . the irrigation ditches, the solid houses, the wide-streeted, sleepy towns. Especially you see the characteristic trees, long lines of them along ditches, along streets, as boundaries between fields and farms . . . These are the "Mormon trees," Lombardy poplars.[13]

(Note the stress on intense green vegetation, order and linear rigidity of the scene, and the substantial nature of house and village.)

Maurine Whipple, in *This Is The Place; Utah,* attempted to deal with the early Mormon landscape in poetic terms:

Already Brigham [Young] saw the trees neat as marching soldiers serried across the land—long lines of Lombardy poplars grouped like pointed spears, cottonwood branches delicate as cobwebs against a winter sky. Already he saw the green of alfalfa checkerboarding sage-gray miles. Already he saw the colonies radiating out from Salt Lake City, . . . Mormon villages trooping down the rivers and irrigable valleys, cuddling at the mouths of canyons under the stored snows. It came to be a landscape pattern as characteristic as a Mormon coat-of-arms . . .[14]

Again a stress on the intense green of irrigated land, the verticality of the poplars, and rectangularity of settlement pattern.

The American writer Thomas Wolfe had an opportunity to travel through "Mormon Country" on his hurried tour of National Parks in the West in 1938. His impressions were vivid, his dislike for the Mormon religion intense, and this pervades his writings. Yet he marvelled at their works. He stereotyped Mormon country along Highway 89 between Kanab and Richfield, Utah, in this way:

Still semi desert with occasional flings into riper green . . . and fields strewn with cut mounds of green lemon hay, and water—the miraculousness of water in the west, the muddy viscousness of irrigation ditches filled with water so incredibly wet . . . and then the dusty little Mormon villages . . . and the forlorn little houses—sometimes just little cramped and

warped wooden boxes, all unpainted, hidden under the mer-
ciful screenings of the dense and sudden trees . . . sometimes
the older Mormon houses of red brick—sometimes still more
ancient ones of chinked log—sometimes strangely an old
Mormon house of stone . . . but of architecture graceless,
all denuded, with the curious sterility and coldness and frus-
tration the religion has—but the earth meanwhile burgeon-
ing into green and fat fertility—the windbreaks of the virgin
poplars, the dense cool green of poplars in the hot bright
light . . . hemmed by the desert peaks—the hackled ridges
on both sides—denuded and half barren, curiously thrilling
in their nakedness . . .[15]

Wolfe's impressionistic interpretations are poignant, even if
markedly subjective. He stresses the harsh desert with its blaz-
ing fierceness, the ditch, and striking green of the oasis. He
acknowledges that there is something different about Mormon settlements. His descriptions of the "tasteless" architecture coupled with mastery over the desert run for pages.
He was also particularly impressed by the Lombardy poplars,
the "lines and windbreaks of incredible poplars" and "the
lightness of new brick—the stamped hard patterns of new
bungalows—and in the bright hot light clear wide streets,
neat houses"[16] of the small settlements closer to Salt Lake
City.

It is clear by now that writers of very different persuasions
have selected or abstracted certain common elements as typical of Mormon landscape. An obvious feeling one gets from
all this is the tremendous contrast between settled, green, cultivated land and the rugged arid land surrounding it. Another
writer tells us that:

Nothing could be more refreshing than a sudden encounter
with a broad green stretch of this kind after miles across arid
wastes where one begins to imagine meadows, farms and
shady brooks to be mere phantasmagoria—when, lo! a magic
turn of the road reveals a sweep of emerald with ditches of
dashing water, plume-like poplars of Lombardy, fan-spread-

ing cottonwoods, vineyards, roses, peach and apple orchards, fig-trees, long lines of acanthus, and all the surroundings of comfortable country life. Again a turn, and the mellow beauty vanishes—not a drop of water then anywhere in sight.[17]

Whipple was referring to this vegetated vs. arid, or fertile vs. sterile dichotomy characteristic of Mormon scenes when she noted the "Biblical peace of tiny green oases set against the savage violence of the hills."[18] The Mormon landscape is, to travelers, truly one of the desert-garden complex. The desert may have "blossomed as the rose" in areas where the Mormons settled, but there is always the "desert" untamed as a framework for Mormon settlements. The German geographer H. Lautensach noted the contrast between riparian poplars and the desert: "The combination of the dark-leaved summer green tree rows with the desert-steppe is a specific characteristic of Mormon land."[19]

These descriptions, repetitious as they are, are typical, and the reader by now has a clear traveler's view of Mormon country. A numerical count of the elements stressed in many descriptions appears in Figure 48. Architecture, poplars and the ubiquitous ditch have left the principal impressions on travelers and observers. The wide streets, shade trees and trees lining streets are second favorites, along with orchards, and rugged mountain backdrop. Gardens, pastures and barns appear to be of tertiary importance in verbal descriptions.

These were the very elements which today typify Canaanville, but the descriptions lack, in general, a sense of the uniqueness with which the elements are combined to form the composite Mormon landscape. All of these elements, with the exception of the hay derrick and certain other rural structures, may be encountered outside of Mormon country. Verbal descriptions can take us only so far. We will remember that the eye was to be the primary tool in analyzing the landscape. The artist is, in this sense, better able to depict the scenery of Mormon country.

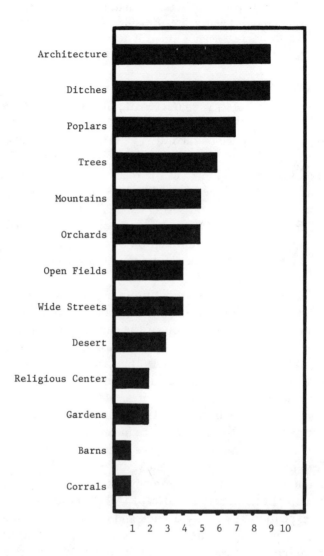

Figure 48.—Elements Stressed in Descriptions of Mormon Settlement.

THE LANDSCAPE ON CANVAS

It is curious that no work has been written on the Mormon landscape in art, nor even a historical study of Utah landscapes and landscape painters. The rural landscape and townscape has been completely neglected, not by artists, but by scholars. Therefore, a brief history of the Mormon landscape in art follows.

A number of fine artists—Mormon and Gentile alike—have dealt with the cultural and physical landscapes of Utah and other parts of the West. J. Haseltine has stated that "the land itself—the crystal atmosphere, the great dome of sky, the spectacular rock formations, the contrasts of lushness and aridity—turned many to landscape painting."[20]

Just a few years after settlement of Salt Lake City, drawings and paintings were executed in Utah to record historical events. The United States Army contracted with several artists to paint and draw scenery; most recorded landforms and the physical setting, a few recorded settlements such as early Salt Lake City. The Mormon Church itself employed its own artists to paint landscapes for the temple interior and other religious buildings, but these were not of Mormon scenes in the West; rather, they were idealized scenes.

The Mormon artists Dan Weggeland (1827-1918) has been called "the father of Utah painting." He was one of the earliest to record Utah on canvas, in a simple, factual style that perhaps revealed his European heritage. His landscape painting entitled *Estate of Brigham Young from the North,* completed in 1868, clearly shows a solid barn, orchard, fences of various types, an early hay derrick and large hay stack, the canal, and a meeting house on the public square. Other Weggeland paintings record the growth of Salt Lake City and environs. During what D.W. Smedley has called the Mormon Period, a fairly faithful representation of landscapes was painted by many artists.[21]

Other, later, artists also painted landscapes, and were more responsive to artistic trends of their times, and less affected by the church. T. Harwood (1860-1940) painted in a pointillistic manner mountains, streams, orchards, and other landscape subjects. George Martin Ottinger (1833-1917) and John Hafen (1856-1910) also painted landscapes, but they too remained interested for the most part in natural settings.[22] The bold physical landscape, with lofty ranges, natural bridges and the like, often obscured the less impressive, pastoral Mormon scenery.

Mahonri Young (1877-1957), however, dealt with landscapes having much cultural content. He has been neglected as a Utah painter, though his prints have recently received attention. Brigham Young University has a fine undisplayed collection of some of his paintings. He captured the Mormon landscape, its shabby farm buildings, Lombardy poplars, little solid homes, and lovely mountains (Figs. 49 and 50). The poplars in Figure 49 are a composition which appears repeatedly in Mormon art from the latter days of the last century until the present.

Edwin Evans (1860-1946) also focused on the Mormon landscape, and his paintings exhibit a Parisian influence. It has been noted that "Evans worked with economy of line with every brush stroke having its meaning."[23] His Red Mountain, painted in the 1930's, depicts a typical Mormon valley in Utah (Fig. 51). The bold, creased red massif looming above a fertile valley punctuated by Lombardy poplars and other trees is, of course, a common scene throughout the Mormon West. He was fond of painting rural landscapes: Old barns (Fig. 52) solid homes and poplars appear to be some of his favorite subjects.

Le Conte Stewart (born 1891) has devoted much of his life to painting western and Mormon scenery. "His boyhood experiences in Richfield and vicinity furnished many impressions which persist to this day."[24] His paintings are almost impressionistic. In some winter scenes, as in Early Spring (Fig. 53) painted in March of 1920, mountains are swelling forms and bare branches are gauze-like, obscuring the homes which they surround. The spectral uniformity of tone is revealed by the difficulty in reproducing this painting in black and white.

Figure 49.—Untitled Landscape Painting of Poplars by Mahonri Young.
The basic composition of Lombardy Poplars silhouetted against moun-
tains and sky is a dominant one in Mormon art. (Courtesy Art Gallery,
Brigham Young University)

Figure 50.—Untitled Landscape Painting of a Farmyard by Mahonri
Young. Probably done about 1910, this captures the rustic quality of a
Mormon farmyard in the snow. (Courtesy Art Gallery, Brigham Young
University)

Figure 51.—Painting Entitled *Red Mountain* by Edwin Evans. (Courtesy Utah Institute of Fine Arts).

Figure 52.—Untitled Water Color of a Barn by Edwin Evans. (Courtesy Art Gallery, Brigham Young University).

Figure 53.—Painting Entitled *Early Spring* by LeConte Stewart. (Courtesy Utah Institute of Fine Arts).

Figure 54.—Painting Entitled *End Of Winter* by Paul Smith. (Courtesy Utah Institute of Fine Arts)

A typical Mormon hay barn, corral, and post and rail fence complex can be seen in Paul S. Smith's 1939 work *End of Winter* (Fig. 54). This water color captures the rustic quality of Mormon "farm" structures, and the unruly appearance of trees in the village landscape.

Many lesser-known artists have discovered the charms of the Mormon landscape. Paintings of rural and village scenery appear frequently in the Mormon West. Usually the artist is not aware that he is painting "Mormon" scenery. Rather, he finds a particular subject colorful or interesting.

Until recently the cultural landscape has been neglected for physical scenes, even in folk art. This is changing. The neglect that has characterized the Mormon landscape has been superseded by a curious interest in the colorful, the ancient, or the rustic. Many a Mormon town and its old buildings are being recorded on canvas for the first time. The movement has both folk and academic roots. There is a growing interest in "old barns" and homes as subject matter for paintings at the art department at Brigham Young University.

COMPOSITION AND TEXTURE

The Mormon landscape has been represented by artists of different "schools" or styles of painting. We therefore find the same landscape being represented differently through time. Nevertheless, certain themes are dominant, and demand discussion. Trevor Southey, a young Mormon artist from Rhodesia, has dealt with Mormon symbolism in art, and has also painted some striking landscapes. He perhaps characterized the feelings of many artists when he noted that the cultural and physical setting in Mormon valleys reflects a "harmony between man and nature." Mormon domestic architecture has a solid, permanent quality; the barn and shed surfaces have developed patinas which bring out the rich textures of natural elements working on hewn and sawn wood. The fascination with the bold forms and masses of barns which can be noted throughout the entire United States has especially fertile ground in Utah. The basic landscape, in addition, is gentle—earthen or old wooden—and nothing is garish, bright or inorganic.

The Mormon landscape offers, too, arrangements and elements for bold compositions, and artists have long capitalized on this. When framed, ground level horizon is often set only one-third of the way from the bottom, while mountains often fill another third, thus terminating in a skyline about one-third of the way from the top—or even higher. Linking these two horizons, and stressing the verticality, are the Lombardy poplars, or sometimes other trees. Occasionally, poplars will thrust above the mountain skyline, and unite earth and sky, foreground and infinity.

Architectural elements can serve the purpose of stressing either the horizontal or vertical. Taller, steeper forms—such

Figure 55.—Elements in the Mormon Landscape Composition.

as houses, chimneys, some barns, and the chapel steeple, stress verticality. Low, rambling forms, such as sheds, fences (especially post and rail fences), ditches and wide roads, stress horizontality. They link compositions in the cross plane and mitigate the pull of vertical elements. Of course the actual horizon lines tend to do this, but since the masses that they demarcate occupy considerable vertical distance, full, bold compositions are the result. The eye is free to wander high into the picture (Fig. 55).

The basic composition is thus a series of horizontal and vertical masses and lines. Both the landscape, and paintings of it, offer reassuring horizontal planes with which to relate. Sharp differences in local relief, however, tend to separate ground level from ultimate horizon. The distance between these two horizontal planes is often large. Accentuating this, and yet linking all together, is a series of vertical elements

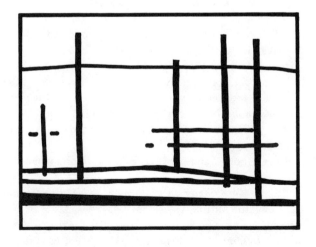

Figure 56.—The Basic Composition of the Mormon Landscape.

that are indeed exclamation points. The composition can in fact be abstracted into a bold grid, slightly and significantly attenuated by verticality (Fig. 56).

What the church and steeple accomplish in both symbolic and psychological terms, by offering a sprawling form and yet leading the eye toward heaven, the Mormon landscape accomplishes by a series of natural and cultural elements. This totality of composition is an important part of the feeling of Mormon Country. The artist is certain to feel this, but the average citizen of Zion may never think in such abstract terms. How he feels about it, however, is of utmost interest to our study. Thus, the next subject to be considered relates to the awareness of the Mormon landscape, not on the literary or artistic level, but among the folk in small villages and towns such as Canaanville.

NOTES

1. J. Schiel, *The Land Between: Dr. James Schiel's Account of the Gunnison-Beckworth Expedition into the West, 1853-1854,* trans. and ed. by Frederick W. Bachmann and William S. Wallace (Los Angeles: Westernlore Press, 1957), pp. 113-114.

2. W. Mulder and A. R. Mortensen, *Among The Mormons: Historic Accounts by Contemporary Observers* (New York: Alfred A. Knopf, 1958), p. 345.

3. Mulder and Mortensen, pp. 330, 332.

4. Nibley, *Brigham Young,* p. 363.

5. R. B. West, *Kingdom of the Saints: The Story of Brigham Young and the Mormons* (New York: Viking Press, 1957), p. 198.

6. D. Evans, "Pioneer Day Events Mark 'Wedding' Anniversary," *Deseret News,* July 24, 1969, p. 2B.

7. J. E. Ricks, "Forms and Methods of Early Mormon Settlement," pp. 26-27.

8. F. A. Bailey, *My Summer In a Mormon Village* (Boston and New York: Houghton Mifflin, 1894), pp. 3-4.

9. A. Jenson, Manuscript History of Snowflake, Arizona, (as quoted from *The Deseret News,* February, 1894) Salt Lake City: Church Historian's Office.

10. *Deseret News,* June 5, 1903, p. 2.
11. C. Johnson, *Highways and Byways of the Rocky Mountains* (New York: The MacMillan Company, 1910), p. 158.
12. J. E. Spencer, "The Development of Agricultural Villages in Southern Utah," *Agricultural History,* Vol. 14 (1940), p. 184.
13. Stegner, *Mormon Country,* p. 21.
14. M. Whipple, *This Is The Place: Utah* (New York: Alfred A. Knopf, 1945), pp. 31-32.
15. T. Wolfe, *A Western Journal: A Daily Log of the Great Parks Trip, June 20-July 2, 1938* (Pittsburgh: University of Pittsburgh Press, 1951), pp. 32-34.
16. Wolfe, pp. 40, 35.
17. G. W. James, *Utah, The Land of Blossoming Valleys* (Boston: The Page Company, 1922), pp. 25-26.
18. Whipple, *This Is the Place,* p. 84.
19. Lautensach, *Das Mormonenland,* p. 30.
20. James L. Haseltine, *100 Years of Utah Painting* (Salt Lake City: Salt Lake Tribune, 1965), p. 9.
21. D. W. Smedley, "An Investigation of Influences on Representative Examples of Mormon Art" (unpublished M.A. Thesis, University of Southern California, 1939), p. 89.
22. Leek, "A Circumspection of Ten Formulators," pp. 39-41, 18-34.
23. Leek, p. 55.
24. P. F. Jacobson, *Golden Sheaves From a Rich Field, A Centennial History of Richfield, Utah, 1864-1964* (Richfield: Richfield Reaper Publishing Company, 1964), p. 161.

CHAPTER 5

The Latter-Day Saint Today
and His Awareness
of the Landscape

We have seen what type of landscape characterizes the
Mormons and have delved into deliberate and even uncon-
scious motivation in its creation. We have seen what authors
and artists represented as the Mormon landscape. The last
questions to be answered are: How do contemporary Latter-
day Saints view the environment created by their predeces-
sors? Are they, as a rule, aware of the landscape that is unique
to their people?

A sociologist some years ago studied the Mormons as a
group. He reported, in reference to the Mormons and their
environment:

> They feel the West to be their own peculiar homeland, pre-
> pared for them by the providential action of Almighty God,
> and its landscape is intimately associated with their self-con-
> sciousness and identified with their past.[1]

Unfortunately, no further references are made in this work to
the landscape or the Mormons' perception and interpretation
of it; yet the statement was for the most part true. And more
than that, there is even an awareness of the uniqueness of
Mormon settlement by non-Mormons who live on the fringes
of Mormon Country.

SOME QUESTIONS AND ANSWERS

For a geographer, delving into the psychological awareness of landscape is a risky undertaking at best, but it is felt that the method used was effective, practical, and accurate. A rich folklore associated with things Mormon emerged from the questionnaire, which sought to elicit frank, spontaneous comments (see questionnaire, Figs. 57-59). Two hundred and twenty people completed the questionnaires, which were administered in interview fashion. People were randomly selected as the town study was being made. They were common folk of various ages. These represent viewpoints from twenty towns, mostly Mormon but some were non-Mormon (Fig. 60). At least ten people were interviewed in each town.

The first questions were of a general nature. Most people felt the places in which they were living were attractive. They mostly liked the mountains and the town-farm atmosphere. The natural scenery or friendly town atmosphere (question two) was usually stressed as being unique. Question three revealed that the Mormons are for the most part quite aware that the early settlers came to the area for "religious freedom," that they were of course LDS, and that they were "hard workers" seeking homes rather than "striking it rich."

When asked if the Mormons actually settled the land any differently than non-Mormons did, many felt that they had not. Those who felt that the Mormons did settle the land differently generally cited the orderly laying out of towns, wide streets, irrigation ditches, chapels, etc. (Fig. 61). Only about 25% of the people who were questioned, however, were consciously then thinking about specific differences in "landscape." From this first part of the questionnaire it would seem that the Mormons as a group do not think about their landscape as being different. But that is because these abstract concepts gave them little or nothing with which to relate.

A tremendous transformation in attitude occurred when people were shown photos of "Town A and Town B," and were asked several questions about them (see Figs. 58 and 59).

1. It has been said that this area is a beautiful and distinctive part of the West. What do you find attractive, or unattractive, about the area in which you live?

2. Is there anything unique about the area in which you live?

3. Was there anything different about the early settlers here when compared to other parts of the West?

4. Do you think that the Mormons have settled the land any differently than others? That is, is there anything different about the scenery of an area settled by them?

5. If so, what parts of the landscape would you consider to be a heritage of the Mormons?

6. The photographs you are looking at were taken in various parts of the West.....

   a) which scene (town) do you find the most attractive? (why?)

   b) which scene (town) reminds you most of "home?" (why?)

   c) which scene (town) might most resemble an area settled by Mormons? (why?)

7. If you are a Mormon (and a farmer), do you continue to work the land with any sense of religious tradition in mind?

8. Do you find landscape as we have been discussing it to be an important part of your daily life?   Or, something which you really don't think too much about?

date_____

location_____

_____

THANK YOU!

male.   female.

age_____   LDS? yes___ no___

Figure 57.—The Questionnaire.

1

2

Figure 58.—"Town A," the Non-Mormon Town.

3

4

1

2

Figure 59.—"Town B," the Mormon Town.

3

4

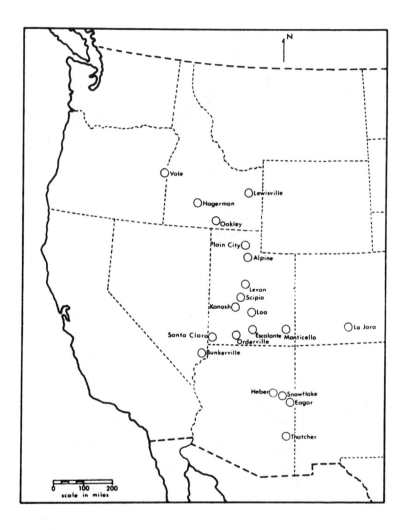

Figure 60.—Selected Towns in the Western United States in Which Questionnaires Were Given.

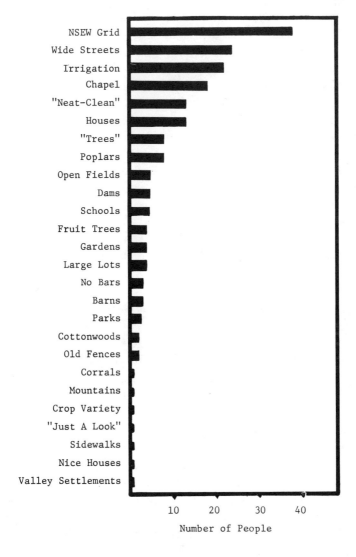

Figure 61.—Elements Cited as Mormon before Photos Were Seen.

The four photos in Town A, it is felt, represent a non-Mormon town rather well. They were taken in the Camp Verde (Fig. 58, photos 1 and 2), and Cottonwood (Fig. 58, photos 3 and 4), Arizona areas. These towns were established in the 1860's and 1870's, and have depended in part on an agricultural base. Town B, on the contrary, is representative of Mormon Country as I have defined it. The photos at Nephi, Utah (Fig. 59, photos 3 and 4) show typical LDS domestic architecture, barns, ditch, etc. Photos 1 and 2 (Fig. 59) show Fountain Green, Utah and include spacious setting, poplars, LDS chapel, etc. Interestingly, the traditional LDS concepts of N-S-E-W grid and wide paved street were not included. Photos of these towns "broke the ice." People enjoyed looking at these "anonymous" towns, and immediately began making comments about them.

A few people immediately suggested, before any questions were asked, that "This one (Town B) is a Mormon town." They could tell, they said by the "Mormon house" (central-hall type), the irrigation ditch and the "Mormon fence." Most people waited until I asked them further questions, however, before giving the answers!

When asked which is the most attractive town, there was a tendency to choose Town A, many people citing the "nice houses" in A, or its "clean look." Those who chose B often cited its farm-like quality as being attractive.

When asked which town most resembled "home," there was in the Mormon towns more agreement that Town B resembled theirs, "because of this old house, we have this kind here," or "because of the barn here," or similar. There was no clear trend, however, toward picking the Mormon town.

The last question, "Which scene (town) might most resemble an area settled by the Mormons?" brought out the most enthusiastic and uniform response. A majority, 78%, chose the correct "town." Why they did so is extremely interesting. The reasons are listed in Fig. 62, "Recognition of landscape elements."

Interestingly, some of those who chose Town B could not say why: "It just looks like a Mormon town," or, "It has the feeling about it." Most, however, were quite specific: "Why, this house here is a polygamy house," said one informant at Snowflake, Arizona. "They had a chimney for each wife." Another theory is that the two doors which are sometimes seen on the front of a house are sure signs of a "polygamy house." This, though, is fantasy. The two front door style was common in the eastern United States at the time of the Mormon migration.[2]

A person at Santa Clara, Utah, looking at the same photo of the old house, told me: "This house looks just like Brigham Young's house itself." It soon became apparent that domestic architecture was the most characteristic element in the photos. The central-hall house is called a "Nauvoo-Style" by some, a "polygamy house" by others, and simply a "Mormon house" by still others. There is a very real awareness that the Mormons had "big houses and big families" as one informant stated, and that the central-hall was a type very often built.

Chapel architecture (Fig. 59, photo 1) was the next most mentioned reason why a person chose Town B. "That's an LDS chapel, all right," one informant in Scipio, Utah told me. "They all look alike." It is truly amazing that people could recognize that this was an LDS chapel, for it was more than a block away from the camera! Chapels are indeed a dominant landscape element: the "Mormon style" is immediately recognizable.

To the Mormons, that steeple has deep religious connotations, of course, and as one Mormon writer noted: "The steeple is less important as an architectural achievement than as the embodiment of religious aspiration."[3] The *Improvement Era* has followed similar themes:

> The church spire catches the sun's last flame,
> A blaze of golden light;
> And holds the gleam on its tapering shaft
> A torch for the coming night![4]

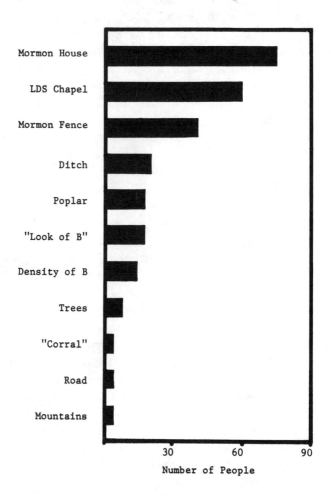

Figure 62.–Recognition of Landscape Elements in "Town B."

The steeple, like the poplars, is a visual exclamation point in the landscape. The sharp vertical break in an otherwise rather horizontally oriented composition is striking. The significance of the chapel in the village landscape should not be underestimated; it has immediate and widespread folk recognition as a Mormon entity.

Totally unexpected was the awareness of the "Mormon fence." It was innocently included as a foreground subject in the same chapel photo. It soon became apparent, however, that in most areas in which the questionnaire was given not only was the term "Mormon fence" used by people to identify it; the fence, as noted, was found to be an important element in the Mormon landscape. "We used to have fences like that here," one informant told me in Kanosh, Utah, as we stood within a few yards of one just like it.

Often informants would choose Town B and start telling me why they thought it was Mormon, and would also tell me they knew where the photos were taken. More often than not they were quite wrong, but correct in the sense that it is extremely difficult to tell exactly where any Mormon photo was taken because of the uniform character of the area as a whole.

Also recognizable, although far less so than the house, chapel or fence, were the irrigation ditch (Fig. 59, photo 3) and the poplar (Fig. 59, photo 2). There is a myth that only the Mormons have irrigation ditches, but the informants were correct in noting that such "gates" are truly characteristic in Mormon towns.

Mormon villagers grow up with the ditch. It is both a symbol of the reality of village agriculture, and a plaything—as we noted at Canaanville. The image is burned into the memory during childhood:

> The irrigation ditch was between the sidewalk and the street and provided water for the surrounding gardens. How we loved that ditch! There was no dearth of activity as long as we could make dams, tiny irrigation systems, waterfalls, water wheels and day dreams with that interesting and fascinating liquid treasure.[5]

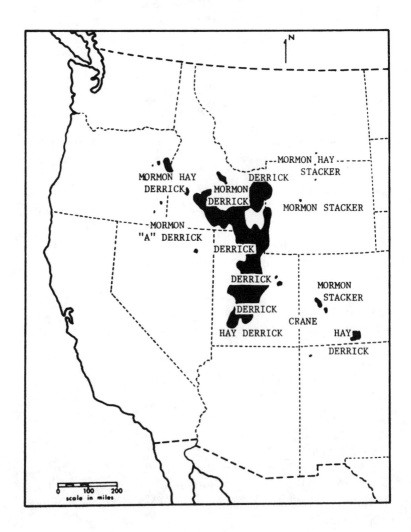

Figure 63.—The Western United States: Names for the Hay Derrick.

Even though the ditch in the photo was concrete-lined, it was familiar to many people in the smallest of towns.

The "Mormon poplar," as it is often called, was cited as being an important clue in identifying Mormon settlements. Sometimes called a Mormon or Lombardy "popular" tree, several informants said the early Mormon pioneers "planted them everywhere they went." The Mormon magazine, *Improvement Era,* has "Mormonized" the poplar. In several articles they have been called "Mormon poplars." Wallace Stegner's *Mormon Country* also "Mormonized" the poplar.

Other traits, too, such as the barn (Fig. 59, photo 3) were considered to be Mormon by some. Several people called them "Mormon barns," but most often they were merely called "old barns." Some said that the "trees" made Town B look like a Mormon town; some people mentioned that corrals and piles of wood, etc., are clues to telling Mormon towns. Others said the roads in Town B looked Mormon; and others said the mountains behind Town B were typical of a Mormon town.

As we noted, some could only say that they chose Town B because it just "looks" Mormon. Others added that the spacing of buildings and the openness of the town told them it was Mormon. All of these clues or elements are things that people used to identify the Mormon town, proving again that there is not only a unique landscape, but a real awareness of it at the folk level.

Not shown in the photos, but closely associated with the Mormons, is the hay derrick. In towns which had hay derricks nearby, people were questioned: "What is that boom and pole device I've seen in fields and pastures that looks like it would be used to swing hay around with?" In the heart of Mormon Country, response was usually, "Oh, you mean the hay derrick." Toward the fringes of the region it was called, however, the "Mormon derrick" or "Mormon stacker" (Fig. 63). These folk terms strongly point to the Mormons as the main agents in the invention and diffusion of the derrick. Studied in terms of modifications of the original forms, the hay derrick appears

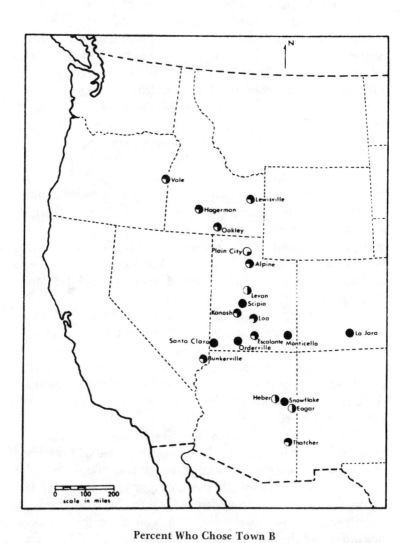

Figure 64.—Selected Towns in the Western United States: Awareness of "Town B" as a Mormon Town.

to be a Mormon element intimately associated with the haying economy of the Great Basin.[6] Folk terminology illustrates a real awareness of it as a Mormon trait.

These conversations, and the photo identifications, were important indicators that people could "sense" Mormon landscape. The mayor of Thatcher, Arizona (LDS) told me, "Your Town B is a Mormon town. Look at the houses and this chapel." He then added, "I can tell a Mormon town just by driving in, going to the center of town, and driving around the block once."

There was, interestingly, very little regional differentiation in the recognition of the Mormon town (Fig. 64). The lowest readings, however, were confined to the central area of the study, fairly close to the "core" in the Utah villages of Levan and Plain City. As a rule, a high percentage of people in both Mormon and non-Mormon towns could choose the correct town using LDS images.

Those people living in towns with especially well developed landscape elements, such as the innumerable poplars at Oakley, Idaho, or the red-brick homes at Snowflake, Arizona, often only cited these as "Mormon" and "typical." Usually, however, the informants cited more general traits, such as architecture, chapels, fences, ditches, and poplars in numbers which varied little across the West. It can, therefore, be said that not only the landscape but also the awareness of it varies little across a vast area.

MYTH AND REALITY

Also very interesting to the geographer is why certain people picked the wrong town (Fig. 58, or Town A). What concepts led them to that choice? Their responses revealed some important myths associated with the Mormons and their settlements.

For some reason, Town A appeared "cleaner" to many people, even some who chose Town B. In reality, Town A was not as clean as Town B when litter is considered, but the shabby look of the Mormon town must have had connotations of being "dirtier." Many people who picked Town A did so because " 'A' must be a Mormon town; it's cleaner," as one woman in Levan, Utah told me. A few people even admitted that the houses in Town B looked more familiar, but that the type of building was less important than its neatness or cleanliness. Often I was told that a typical Mormon town was one like Fillmore or Brigham City, Utah—both winners of various "city clean" landscape contests in recent years. The fact that one might have to drive through many Mormon towns of more "rustic" quality to reach these examples was not considered! The clean, well-ordered Mormon town concept appears to relate to both remnants of the City of Zion concept and a basic ethnocentrism involving the Mormons as a superior, cleaner, group.

In two cases the accusation was made, "You have picked photos which are making the Mormons look bad." Both respondents were women. They said that the weedy road shoulders and the old fence in Town B were not typical. Neither, said one woman in Snowflake, Arizona, were the "old houses that no Mormon would live in today." Several people thought that I had selected "old photos" of the Mormon town. They were shocked to learn that the photos were taken within two weeks of each other!

As a rule, most of the people who answered the questionnaire were warm and friendly. Most were intensely interested in the role of their people in settling the West. As there was no real regional differentiation in awareness, neither was there much age variation. The lower limit was about twelve years old, and these youngsters were as often able to pick the correct town as their parents and grandparents.

The question relating to the religious tradition in working the land drew for the most part negative response. Some felt that "some Mormons even today still do," but none were ever encountered. Most farmers felt that they were "trying to make a living" rather than anything else. Others expressed an interesting concept that "everything I do is related to my religious tradition." Rather than having any concept of the City of Zion, however, most were referring to the notion that "when you develop new ways of doing things you become more productive in the eyes of God, and that is our religious tradition."

The Mormons on the fringes of the Mormon culture region especially often feel themselves to be ready acceptors of farming innovations. This is noteworthy, for many of the non-Mormons feel the same way about the Mormons, often praising their good farms and aggressive, economical attitudes. This readiness to accept new ways is responsible in part for the more rapid transformation of the rural landscape at the visual fringe and in Meinig's core area. These changes, however, are slowly finding their way into even the visual nucleus of Mormon Country. Each year new non-Mormon changes are wrought.

The last question drew an almost unanimous response: "Yes, the way our surroundings look is very important to us." Others said, "You can tell the type of people in a town just by looking at it." This is reminiscent of "Ye shall know them by their fruits" (Matthew 7:16). Landscape in this sense becomes a badge of identity as well as a symbol of a type of people. Most people recognized a difference between the real and the ideal ("our town should be cleaner"), but felt a deep sense of religious involvement with their locations. The Mormon towns always stand out as those which were platted by church leaders divinely inspired. "The cause of settling here was religious freedom and our church leaders knew the best places," was a response often made with slight variation.

The awareness of the shabby quality of farms runs high. During World War II there was a joke circulating in Mormon Country:

The West Coast people who are worried about threats of air raids on the coast should live here. No one would ever bomb these Utah towns. Anyone flying over would think they've already been bombed!

And yet, it is often repeated that these farm villages were the result of religious inspiration, and were planned and laid out according to the will of God. The conflict between the real and the ideal runs deep in the mind of the Mormon villager. He is caught between what should be, and what is. He finds, nevertheless, much to identify with. There is a deep sentiment attached to place in the Mormon West.

TOTALITY AND VISION

The concept of landscape is incorporated into an entire life style. Landscape becomes a framework for living, not a consciously perceived entity. Life, land, and landscape become one, as exemplified in this poem praising life in a Mormon village:

A GOOD PLACE TO LIVE

A fine place to live is our Fountain Green Ward
In a high mountain valley revealed by the Lord
To our Pioneer fathers, who with love for their God
And with strength in their hearts, turned over the sod.

Diverted the water, with toil changed the scene
From one of grey sagebrush to fields brightly green
To houses and gardens, to streets wide and straight
To a place filled with friendship—where no one knew hate.

Thus they handed it to us, to live in—enjoy
To rear up our families, where each girl and boy
Can grow strong and clean, like the light of the sun
Can get a good start at life's course to be run.

We are proud of our ward and the town it embraces
With its gem of a park, and the glow of proud faces
As they enter our chapel, so spacious and new
A splendid example of what we can do.

We are farmers and shepherds, industrial men,
School teachers, storekeepers who always know when
To shake a friends hand, to greet with a smile
To work or to play, and to make life worthwhile.

And so it behooves us to keep and to guard
The blessing of living in Fountain Green Ward.[7]

Because of the Mormon town's strict adherence to the grid
pattern, "right with the compass and right with the world" as
citizens may say, and because there are religious connotations
to such land division, the villager's sense of direction is phe-
nomenal. Travel directions are not given in the traditional
"turn left, then right." The Mormon villager says, "turn north,
then east." They repair the "west" wall of the barn, or move
a hay derrick farther "north." Even inside the house, someone may move a painting a "little farther south" on the wall.
The orientation is a vast grid. Landscape is part of the framework. The elements in place give a sense of order.

The mountains, we recall, were the starting point for our
study of Canaanville. To the Mormons, these mountains remain as symbols of both a closeness to God, and fulfillment
of the prophecy of settling in the Rocky Mountains.

Indeed, the citizens of Nephi, Utah regard towering Mt.
Nebo with a sense approaching mysticism. Many Mormons
throughout the West told me of the feeling of "security"
they had in their valley locations, because of the "protection
of the mountains."

This is a theme which reaches far back into Mormon history. We noted that the early Mormon leaders stressed the
protection, isolation, and security of the mountains. As
brother Segmiller told the Bunkerville, Nevada ward in 1897,
". . . the Saints were to be geathered [sic] to the chambers of
the mountains in obedience to counsel."[8] At Clarkston, Utah
the same theme was developed: "Thomas Griffin spoke of us
fulfilling ancient prophecies by living in the mountains and
that we are free from many of the devastation [sic] in the

world." And as recorded in a folk song about Clarkston the same theme dominates:

> Clarkston is our village, yours and mine,
> Cradled in the Rockies, firm and fine.
> Prophets planned its being, long ago.
> It's our town we all love so.[10]

What these verses lack in literary refinement they capture in the folk awareness of security. The early Mormons had many songs dealing with the mountain Zion: "Oh Ye Mountains High," "High on the Mountain Top," "Our Mountain Home So Dear," and "Zion Stands with Hills Surrounded," are but a few. They all deal with the concept of the mountains as protecting barriers.

This spiritual and even material protection is felt today. The setting of the town of Emery, Utah, is described in one book: "The mountains at this point are rugged and majestic and seem to stand as sentinels, guarding the little town."[11]

The basically religious theme has become to some extent secularized. Even in the Mormon version of the old "girl-loses-boy" hardship story the mountains become symbolic of strength and protection. Or, as the final line reads: "She must let her heart be healed by the strength of the mountains beyond."[12] Many people who responded to the questionnaire frankly admitted that the mountains gave them a secure feeling. As one Mormon author noted: "The best way to appreciate mountains is to move where you cannot see them—then you want to get back again."[13]

With the mountains which so often frame the landscape, and which offer a sense of protection to the Latter-day Saints, we bring to a close our study of their perception and interpretation of a unique landscape. The Mormons are themselves aware that they transformed a difficult environment into a distinctive cultural landscape. Landscape is the geographer's term, however, for a deeply subconscious visual framework in which the Mormons operate. Intricately bound to concepts and feelings of place is this visual framework. As patriotism is made concrete with "amber fields" and "purple mountains," nostalgia and love of home, too, are based on a series of visual clues: LDS chapels, Mormon barns, "Nauvoo style" homes, and other elements—all placed in a rigid grid system. Landscape is, therefore, an integral part of the *genre de vie.*

As the Mormon church sought both consciously and subconsciously to create a unique landscape, so today do the Mormons living in their mountain Zion perceive the visual pattern to be very much a part of their culture and their religion. Mormons see everywhere the strengths and weaknesses of their way of life vividly imprinted in bold and striking patterns: fine, solid religious and domestic architecture stands opposed to the run-down quality of almost everything else. And yet, everything is related to their culture, and persists because of it.

Landscape thus becomes an important part of cultural ecology. The images familiar to the Mormons, while they may be joked about by visitors and even Mormons themselves, are in reality a pattern perpetuated by deeply subconscious motivation. This substantiates the generalized hypothesis by Lowenthal and Prince that "landscapes are formed by landscape tastes."[14] Patterns persist because they are treasured, as well as being the result of "neglect." Those patterns, with their inherent solidity, orderliness and contradicting shabbiness are important to the Mormons, and form the unique entity that is the Mormon landscape.

NOTES

1. T. F. O'dea, *The Mormons* (Chicago: University of Chicago Press, 1957), p. 1.
2. Utah folklorist Austin Fife has concluded that there is "unfortunately no correlation between number of wives and number of doors. Besides, additional wives usually lived in separate dwellings." Personal communication, Oct. 25, 1969, Logan, Utah. A similar refutation is found in J. E. Spencer, "House Types of Southern Utah," *Geographical Review,* Vol. 35 (1945), p. 448.

3. D. Hill, "Early Mormon Churches in Utah: A Photographic Essay," *Dialogue: A Journal of Mormon Thought,* Vol. 1 (1966), p. 14.

4. E. Hopper, "The Church Spire," *Improvement Era,* Vol. 63 (1959), p. 271.

5. D. S. Howard, in K. B. Carter's "Pioneer Houses and Enclosures," *Our Pioneer Heritage,* Vol. 1 (1958), p. 136.

6. A. E. Fife and J. M. Fife, "Hay Derricks of the Great Basin and Upper Snake River Valley," *Western Folklore Quarterly,* Vol. 7 (1948), pp. 225-239.

7. Composed by Vance W. Aagard, and read by Ora Peterson at the "Lamb Day-Pioneer Day" historical program at the L.D.S. chapel, Fountain Green, Utah, 10 a.m., July 26, 1969.

8. Historical Record, Bunkerville Ward (St. George Stake), January 11, 1879 to September 22, 1901, p. 47. Salt Lake City, Church Historian's Office.

9. Historical Record, Clarkston Ward (Cache Stake), 1893 to 1899, April 30, 1899, p. 374. Salt Lake City, Church Historian's Office.

10. B. J. Ravsten and E. P. Ravsten, *History of Clarkston, The Granary of Cache Valley.* (Published by the Authors, 1966), p. 31.

11. S. Mc Elprang, *Castle Valley: A History of Emery County* (Emery County Company Daughters of Utah Pioneers, 1949), p. 137.

12. M. Jensen, "And the Mountains Beyond," *Improvement Era,* Vol. 45, (1942), p. 393.

13. L. S. Morris, "Home Beautification," *Improvement Era,* Vol. 32 (1929), p. 463.

14. D. Lowenthal and H. C. Prince, "English Landscape Tastes," *The Geographical Review,* Vol. 55 (1965), p. 186.

Bibliography

Arrington, Leonard J. *Great Basin Kingdom: Economic History of the Latter-Day Saints, 1830-1900.* Lincoln: University of Nebraska Press, 1958.

Bailey, Florence Augusta. *My Summer in a Mormon Village.* Boston and New York: Houghton Mifflin, 1894.

Bangerter, Herman R. "Significance of Ancient, Geometric Symbols." *Temples of the Most High.* Edited by N.B. Lundwall. Salt Lake City: N.B. Lundwall, 1941. pp. 239-242.

Day, Stella H. and Ekins, Sebrina C. *Milestones of Millard: 100 Years of History of Millard County.* Springville: Art City Publishing Co., 1951.

Goeldner, Paul. *Utah Catalog, Historic American Buildings Survey.* Salt Lake City: Utah Heritage Foundation, 1969.

Goodwin, S.H. *Mormonism and Masonry.* Salt Lake City: Grand Lodge, F. & A.M. of Utah, 1938.

Hamlin, Talbot. *Greek Revival Architecture in America.* New York: Oxford University Press, 1944.

Harris, Chauncy Dennison. *Salt Lake City: A Regional Capital.* Chicago: University of Chicago Libraries, 1940.

Haseltine, James L. *100 Years of Utah Painting.* Salt Lake City: Salt Lake Tribune, 1965.

Horne, Alice Merrill. *Devotees and Their Shrines: A Handbook of Utah Art.* Salt Lake City: Deseret News, 1914.

Jacobson, Pearl F. *Golden Sheaves From a Rich Field, A Centennial History of Richfield, Utah, 1864-1964.* Richfield: Richfield Reaper Publishing Company, 1964.

James, George Wharton. *Utah, The Land of Blossoming Valleys.* Boston: The Page Co., 1922.

Johnson, Clifton. *Highways and Byways of the Rocky Mountains.* New York: The MacMillan Company, 1910.

Lautensach, Hermann. *Das Mormonenland als Beispiel eines sozialgeographischen Raumes.* Bonn: Im Selbstverlag des Geographischen Instituts der Universität Bonn, 1953.

Lehner, Ernst. *The Picture Book of Symbols.* New York: William Penn Publishing Corporation, 1956.

Levine, Albert J. *Snowflake: A Pictorial Review, 1878-1964.* Snowflake, Arizona: By the Author, 1965.

Lichten, Frances. *Folk Art of Rural Pennsylvania.* New York: Charles Scribner's Sons, 1946.

McClintock, James H. *Mormon Settlement in Arizona: A Record of Peaceful Conquest of the Desert.* Phoenix: Manufacturing Stationers Inc., 1921.

McCune, Alice Paxman. *History of Juab County: A History Prepared for the Centennial of the Coming of the Pioneers to Utah, 1847-1947.* Springville: Art City Publishing Company, 1947.

McElprang, Stella. *'Castle Valley': A History of Emery County.* Emery County Company of the Daughters of Utah Pioneers, 1949.

Marsh, George Perkins. *Man and Nature.* David Lowenthal, editor. Cambridge: The Belknap Press of Harvard University Press, 1965.

Morgan, Dale L. *Utah: A Guide to the State.* New York: Hastings House, Publishers, 1941.

Mulder, William and Mortensen, A. Russell. *Among the Mormons: Historic Accounts by Contemporary Observers.* New York: Alfred A. Knopf, 1958.

Nelson, Lowry. *The Mormon Village, A Pattern and Technique of Land Settlement.* Salt Lake City: University of Utah Press, 1952.

Newcomb, Rexford. *Architecture of the Old Northwest Territory.* Chicago: University of Chicago Press, 1950.

Nibley, Preston. *Brigham Young, The Man and His Work.* Salt Lake City: Deseret Press, 1937.

O'dea, Thomas F. *The Mormons.* Chicago: University of Chicago Press, 1957.

Ravsten, Ben J. and Ravsten, Eunice P., editors. *History of Clarkston, The Granary of Cache Valley, 1864-1964.* By the editors, 1966.

Reps, John W. *The Making of Urban America: A History of City Planning in the United States.* Princeton: Princeton University Press, 1965.

Reps, John W. *Town Planning in Frontier America.* Princeton: Princeton University Press, 1969.

Schiel, James. *The Land Between: Dr. James Schiel's Account of The Gunnison-Beckworth Expedition Into the West, 1853-1854.* Translated and edited by Frederick W. Bachmann and William S. Wallace. Los Angeles: Westernlore Press, 1957.

Snow, Anne. *Rainbow Views: A History of Wayne County.* Springville: Art City Publishing Company, 1953.

Sopher, David E. *Geography of Religions.* Foundations of Cultural Geography Series. Englewood Cliffs: Prentice-Hall Inc., 1967.

Stegner, Wallace Earle. *Mormon Country.* New York: Duell, Sloane and Pearce, 1942.

West, Ray B. *Kingdom of The Saints: The Story of Brigham Young and the Mormons.* New York: Viking Press, 1957.

Whipple, Maurine. *This Is The Place: Utah.* New York: Alfred A. Knopf, 1945.

Whittlesey, Derwent. "The Regional Concept and the Regional Method." *American Geography—Inventory and Prospect.* Preston James and Clarence Jones, editors. Syracuse: Syracuse University Press, 1954.

Widtsoe, John A. *How the Desert Was Tamed.* Salt Lake City: Deseret Book Company, 1947.

Wolfe, Thomas. *A Western Journal: A Daily Log of the Great Parks Trip, June 20-July 2, 1938.* Pittsburgh: University of Pittsburgh Press, 1951.

Woolsey, Nethella Griffin. *The Escalante Story: A History of the Town of Escalante, and Description of the Surrounding Territory, Garfield County, Utah, 1875-1964.* Springville: Art City Publishing Company, 1964.

REPORTS—PUBLISHED

Relief Society Women's Auxiliary of The Church of Jesus Christ of Latter-day Saints. *A Centenary of Relief Society: 1842-1942.* Salt Lake City: General Board of Relief Society, 1942.

Utah State Institute of Fine Arts. *Report on the Fine Arts in Utah, 1968.* Salt Lake City: University of Utah, June, 1968.

ARTICLES IN JOURNALS AND MAGAZINES

Ashton, Marvin O. "Stop! Look! Listen!" *Improvement Era.* Vol. 46 (September, 1943), pp. 526-527.

Bjorklund, Elaine M. "Ideology and Culture Exemplified in Southwestern Michigan." *Annals, Association of American Geographers.* Vol. 54 (June, 1964), pp. 227-241.

Burton, Harold W. "Our Church Architectural Development." *Improvement Era.* Vol. 62 (April, 1959), pp. 252-267.

Cannon, Lewis T. "Architecture of Church Buildings." *The Improvement Era.* Vol. 17 (May, 1914), pp. 793-801.

Carter, Kate B. "The Mormon Village." *Treasures of Pioneer History.* Vol. 4 (1955), pp. 133-188.

Carter, Kate B. "Pioneer Houses and Enclosures." *Our Pioneer Heritage.* Vol. 1 (1958), pp. 117-187.

Evans, David W., Taylor, James; and Cannon, J. Q. "Discourse by Elder Orson Pratt, Delivered in the New Tabernacle, Salt Lake City, Sunday Afternoon, June 15, 1873." *Journal of Discourses by President Brigham Young, His Counsellors, The Twelve Apostles, and others.* Vol. 16 (1874), pp. 78-87.

Fife, Austin E. and Fife, James M. "Hay Derricks of The Great Basin and Upper Snake River Valley." *Western Folklore Quarterly.* Vol. 7 (July, 1948), pp. 225-239.

Fox, Feramorz Y. "The 'Mormon' Farm Village in Colorado." *The Improvement Era.* Vol. 46 (August, 1943), pp. 451, 497.

Gallois, Lucien. "L'Utah." *Annales de Geographie.* Vol. 22 (1913), pp. 185-196.

Gates, Susa Young. "Reminiscences of Brigham Young." *Improvement Era.* Vol. 11 (June, 1908), pp. 617-624.

Geddes, Jos. A. "Modifications of the Early Utah Farm Village." *Yearbook of the Association of Pacific Coast Geographers.* Vol. 8 (1942), pp. 15-22.

Gibbs, George F., Irvine, John; *et al.* "Discourse by President John Taylor, Delivered at Malad, Oneida County, Idaho, Wednesday Morning, October 20th, 1881." *Journal of Discourses by John Taylor, President of the Church of Jesus Christ of Latter-day Saints, His Counsellors, The Twelve Apostles, and others.* Vol. 26 (1886), pp. 105-113.

Hall, Frances. "Partnership With Trees." *Improvement Era.* Vol. 47 (October, 1944), p. 590.

Hill, Douglas. "Early Mormon Churches in Utah: A Photographic Essay." *Dialogue: A Journal of Mormon Thought.* Vol. 1 (Autumn, 1966), pp. 13-22.

Hopper, Ethel. "The Church Spire." *Improvement Era.* Vol. 62 (April, 1959), p. 271.

Jensen, Melba. "And the Mountains Beyond." *Improvement Era.* Vol. 45 (June, 1942), pp. 379, 392-393.

Leighly, John. "Some Comments on Contemporary Geographic Method." *Annals,* Association of American Geographers. Vol. 27 (September, 1937), pp. 125-141.

Lillibridge, Robert M. "Architectural Currents on the Mississippi River Frontier: Nauvoo, Illinois." *Journal of the Society of Architectural Historians.* Vol. 19 (October, 1960), pp. 109-114.

Lowenthal, David and Prince, Hugh C. "English Landscape Tastes." *The Geographical Review.* Vol. 55 (April, 1965), pp. 186-222.

McKay, David O. "The Purpose of the Temples." *Improvement Era.* (Temple Issue: Temples and Latter-day Saints) n.d., pp. 2-8.

Meinig, Donald W. "The Mormon Culture Region: Strategies and Patterns in the Geography of the American West, 1847-1964." *Annals,* Association of American Geographers. Vol. 55 (June, 1965), pp. 191-220.

Morris, L. S. "Home Beautification." *Improvement Era.* Vol. 32 (April, 1929), pp. 460-465.

Mulder, William. "The Mormons in American History." *Bulletin of the University of Utah.* Vol. 48, (No. 11, January 14, 1957).

Olson, John Alden. "Proselytism, Immigration and Settlement of Foreign Converts to the Mormon Culture in Zion." *Journal of the West.* Vol. 6 (April, 1967), pp. 189-204.

Price, Edward T. "Viterbo: Landscape of an Italian City." *Annals,* Association of American Geographers. Vol. 54 (June, 1964), pp. 242-275.

Price, Edward T. "A Geography of Color." *Geographical Review.* Vol. 54 (October, 1964), pp. 590-592.

Ricks, Joel Edward. "Forms and Methods of Early Mormon Settlement in Utah and the Surrounding Region." *Utah State University Monograph Series.* Vol. 11 (No. 2, January, 1964).

Seeman, Albert L. "Communities in the Salt Lake Basin." *Economic Geography.* Vol. 14 (July, 1938), pp. 300-308.

Sellers, Charles L. "Early Mormon Community Planning." *Journal of the American Institute of Planners.* Vol. 28 (February, 1962), pp. 24-30.

Smith, Henry C. "City Planning." *Journal of History.* Vol. 15 (January, 1922), pp. 1-17.

Solomon, R. J. "Procedures In Townscape Analysis." *Annals, Association of American Geographers.* Vol. 56 (June, 1966), pp. 254-268.

Spencer, Joseph Earle. "The Development of Agricultural Villages in Southern Utah." *Agricultural History.* Vol. 14 (1940), pp. 181-189.

Spencer, Joseph Earle. "House Types of Southern Utah." *Geographical Review.* Vol. 35 (July, 1945), pp. 444-457.

Tanner, Joseph M. "Architecture in Religion." *The Improvement Era.* Vol. 17 (May, 1914), pp. 789-791.

Watt, G. D. "The Devil To Be Cast Out of the Earth - The Emigration Fund—Exhortation to Bishops—Laying Up Stores Against a Time of Need. A Discourse by President Heber C. Kimball, Delivered in the Tabernacle, Great Salt Lake City, March 9, 1856." *Journal of Discourses by Brigham Young, President of the Church of Jesus Christ of Latter-day Saints, His Two Counsellors, The Twelve Apostles, and others.* Vol. 3 (1856), pp. 249-254.

Watt, G. D.; and Long, J. V. "Prosperity of Zion &c., Discourse Delivered by Elder George A. Smith, in the Tabernacle, Great Salt Lake City, March 10, 1861." *Journal of Discourses Delivered by President Brigham Young, His Two Counsellors, The Twelve Apostles, and others.* Vol. 9 (1862), pp. 66-75.

Zelinsky, Wilbur. "An Approach to the Religious Geography of the United States: Patterns of Church Membership in 1952." *Annals, Association of American Geographers.* Vol. 51 (June, 1961), pp. 139-193.

ARTICLES IN NEWSPAPERS

Anderson, Stan. "Utah Has Snubbed a Friend." *The Salt Lake Tribune.* September 6, 1953. pp. 8m-9m, p. 14.

Deseret News, April 29, 1851, p. 38.

Deseret News. June 5, 1903, p. 2.

Deseret News. "Distinctive Style of Church Architecture Developed." December 17, 1921, p. 29.

Evans, DeAnn. "Pioneer Day Events Mark 'Wedding' Anniversary." *Deseret News.* Thursday, July 24, 1969. pp. B-1, B-2.

Mitchell, Robert C. "Obscure Spring City Utah Williamsburg?" *Deseret News.* March 11, 1968, pp. 5-7.

Nelson, Ray. "Makes Appeal for Old Things." *The Herald Journal* (Logan, Utah), November 13, 1969, p. 2.

Patrick, William C. "Poplar Trees Are Happiest." *The Salt Lake Tribune.* November 12, 1950, Section M, p. 1m.

Richards, Stephen L. "Chapels and Temples Held Monuments to Progress of Man." *Deseret News,* October 25, 1953, pp. 1-3.

MANUSCRIPT COLLECTIONS

LDS = Church Historian's Office, Archives, Church of Jesus Christ of Latter-day Saints, Salt Lake City, Utah.

UHS = Utah Historical Society, Historical Records, Salt Lake City, Utah.

"Brigham Young, Letter to Pres. Ezra Benson and Bp. Peter Maughan, from Wellsville to Logan, Utah. August 7, 1865," Utah Historical Society. Files; Peter Maughan Papers. (UHS)

Bunkerville (Nevada) Ward, St. George Stake, Historical Record, January 11, 1879 to September 22, 1901. (LDS)

Clarkston (Utah) Ward, Cache Stake, Historical Records, 1893 to 1899. (LDS)

Eagar (Arizona) Ward, Record of Sunday Services and Priesthood Meetings of the Union Ward, 1888-1894. (LDS)

Escalante (Utah) Ward, Garfield Stake, Historical Record, 1892-1900. (LDS)

Jenson, Andrew. Snowflake (Arizona) Ward Manuscript History. n.d. (LDS)

Loa (Utah) Ward, Wayne Stake, Historical Record, 1894-1898. (LDS)

Manassa (Colorado) Ward, San Luis Stake, Historical Record (and Record of Members), Book A, 1877-1879. (LDS)

Nephi (Utah) Ward, Juab Stake, Record of Members (1852-1854) and Historical Record (1851-1862). (LDS)

Nephi (Utah), Conferences and Meetings, Nephi Branch, Historical Record and Record of Members, 1855-1862. (LDS)

Nephi (Utah), Juab County, Farmers and Gardners Club, 1883-1894. (LDS)

Owens, David Kerns. Nov. 16, 1938. Pioneer Personal Interview with Henry Excell. Utah State Historical Society. WPA Questionnaire Files. (UHS)

Parowan (Utah) Stake, Historical Records, 1856-1859. (LDS)

Rice, Clayton. "Thoughts, Experiences, and Stories of Others in Utah."
    Diary no. 1, from July 10, 1908 to November 29, 1909. Unpub-
    lished manuscript, University of Oregon Special Collection.
St. George Gardners Club, Agreement. February 16, 1873, 7 pp. Unpub-
    lished document. Utah Historical Society, Historical Files. (UHS)
Snowflake (Arizona) Ward, Historical Record, Book C, 1888-1891.
    (LDS)
Wayne (Utah) Stake, Historical Records, 1895-1901. (LDS)

UNPUBLISHED MATERIALS

Baum, John Haws. "Geographical Characteristics of Early Mormon Set-
    tlement." Unpublished M.A. Thesis, Brigham Young University,
    1967.
DeGraw, Monte Bowen. "A Study of Representative Examples of Art
    Works Fostered by the Mormon Church With an Analysis of the
    Aesthetic Values of These Works." Unpublished M.A. Thesis, Brig-
    ham Young University, 1959.
Dougall, Patricia. "The Shade Trees of Salt Lake City, Utah." Unpub-
    lished M.S. Thesis, University of Utah, 1942.
Gleave, Ray Haum. "The Effect of the Speaking of George A. Smith on
    the People of the Iron Mission of Southern Utah." Unpublished
    M.A. Thesis, Brigham Young University, 1957.
Layton, Robert. "The Mormon Village." Paper presented at the Great
    Plains-Rocky Mountain Section of the Association of American Ge-
    ographers, Salt Lake City, Utah. October 10, 1969.
Leek, Thomas A. "A Circumspection of Ten Formulators of Early Utah
    Art History." Unpublished M.A. Thesis, Brigham Young Univer-
    sity, 1961.
Markham, Fred L. "Early Architecture, 1847-1870." Unpublished
    manuscript, Utah Historical Society, 1963.
Peterson, Charles Sharon. "Settlement on the Little Colorado, 1873-
    1900: A Study of the Processes and Institutions of Mormon Ex-
    pansion." Unpublished Ph.D. dissertation, University of Utah,
    1967.
Smedley, Delbert Waddoups. "An Investigation of Influences on Rep-
    resentative Examples of Mormon Art." Unpublished M.A. Thesis,
    University of Southern California, 1939.

Spencer, Deloy. "A History of Escalante." Unpublished Manuscript, Utah Historical Society, 1960.

Spencer, Joseph Earle. "The Middle Virgin River Valley, Utah: A Study in Cultural Growth and Change." Unpublished Ph.D. dissertation, University of California, 1936.

Wilcox, Keith Wilson. "An Architectural Design Concept for the Church of Jesus Christ of Latter-day Saints." Unpublished M.A. Thesis, University of Oregon, 1953.

Winburn, David. "The Early Homes of Utah: A Study of Techniques and Materials." Unpublished B.A. Thesis, University of Utah, 1952.

Yonemori, Shirley Kazuko. "Mahonri Mackintosh Young, Printmaker." Unpublished M.A. Thesis, Brigham Young University, 1963.

Index